Be a
Christ-Focused
Small Group Leader

A handbook for leading a
women's small group

Melanie Newton

JOYFUL
WALK
MINISTRIES

This is the revised version of the handbook, *The 5 C's of Small Group Leadership*, first developed by the wonderful women who served the Lord as Bible Study small group leaders over the years at Crossroads Bible Church in Double Oak, TX. Many thanks go to the lessons I learned from them about leading a small group. Also, thanks to Barbie Thrasher who was part of that group of leaders and carefully edited this revised version.

Be a Christ-Focused Small Group Leader: A handbook for leading a women's small group

Published by Joyful Walk Press. Flower Mound, TX.

ISBN: 979-8-9925750-9-5

For questions about the use of this handbook or to order bulk copies, please email us at melanienewton.com/contact.

The graphic used on the cover is a public domain image (53e9b33b-c92d-4397-814d-8eeb163b9d65.jpg). The picture reminds me that a small group leader waters what God has planted and makes to grow.

Melanie Newton is the author of "Graceful Beginnings" books for anyone new to the Bible and "Joyful Walk Bible Studies" for established Christians. Her mission is to help women learn to study the Bible for themselves and to grow their Bible-teaching skills to lead others.

We pray that you and your fellow group leaders will find *Be a Christ-Focused Small Group Leader* to be a resource that God will use to strengthen you as a minister to others in a small group.

Grace-based Bible Studies • Always Relevant • Never Fluff

JOYFUL WALK PRESS
Flower Mound, TX

MELANIE NEWTON

Melanie Newton is a Louisiana girl who made the choice to follow Jesus while attending LSU. She and her husband Ron married and moved to Texas for him to attend Dallas Theological Seminary. They stayed in Texas where Ron led a wilderness camping ministry for troubled youth for many years. Ron now helps corporations with their challenging employees and is the author of the top-rated business book, *No Jerks on the Job*.

Melanie jumped into raising three Texas-born children and serving in ministry to women at her church. Through the years, the Lord has given her opportunity to do Bible teaching and to write grace-based Bible studies for women that are now available from her website (melanienewton.com) and on Bible.org. *Graceful Beginnings* books are for anyone new to the Bible. *Joyful Walk Bible Studies* are for maturing Christians.

Melanie loves to help women learn how to study the Bible for themselves. She also teaches online courses for women to grow their Bible-teaching skills to help others—all with the goal of getting to know Jesus more along the way. Her heart's desire is to encourage you to have a joyful relationship with Jesus Christ so you are willing to share that experience with others around you.

> "Jesus took hold of me in 1972, and I've been on this great adventure ever since. My life is a gift of God, full of blessings in the midst of difficult challenges. The more I've learned and experienced God's absolutely amazing grace, the more I've discovered my faith walk to be a joyful one. I'm still seeking that joyful walk every day..."

> *Melanie*

OTHER BIBLE STUDIES BY MELANIE NEWTON

Graceful Beginnings books for anyone new to the Bible:

A Fresh Start (basics for new Christians)
Painting the Portrait of Jesus (the Gospel of John)
The God You Can Know (the character of God)
Grace Overflowing (an overview of Paul's 13 letters)
The Walk from Fear to Faith (7 Old Testament women)
Satisfied by His Love (women who knew Jesus)
Seek the Treasure (study of Ephesians)
Pathways to a Joyful Walk (6 pathways to a joy-filled life)

Joyful Walk Bible Studies for growing Christians:

Adorn Yourself with Godliness (1 Timothy and Titus)
Everyday Women, Ever Faithful God (Old Testament women,)
Connecting Faith to Life on Planet Earth (Genesis 1-11; Revelation)
Graceful Living (the essentials for a grace-based Christian life)
Graceful Living Today Devotional (for a joyful Christian life)
Healthy Living (Colossians and Philemon)
Heartbreak to Hope (the Gospel of Mark)
Identity: Sticking to Your Faith in a Pull-Apart World (Ezra-Malachi)
Knowing Jesus, Knowing Joy (Philippians,)
Live Out His Love (New Testament women)
Perspective (1and 2 Thessalonians)
Profiles of Perseverance (Old Testament men)
Radical Acts (Acts)
Reboot, Renew, Rejoice (1 and 2 Chronicles)
The God-Dependent Woman (2 Corinthians)
To Be Found Faithful (2 Timothy)

Resources for leading others:

Be a Christ-Focused Small Group Leader
Leap into Lifestyle Disciplemaking
Painting the Picture of Jesus (the "I Am's" of Jesus for children)
Teaching Children the God They Can Know (the character of God)

Download our catalogue and get resources for your spiritual growth at melanienewton.com.

CONTENTS

How to Use This Book

Welcome to small group ministry! Small groups provide a great opportunity for women to grow in their faith and to experience authentic, loving relationships with other believers. Your role is to maximize both opportunities for all participants, including yourself.

Women are best equipped for small group ministry through regular training and resources in the "how-to's" of ministry to other believers. In addition, knowing how to use one's unique design, spiritual gifts, and calling will enrich the ministry within the Body of Christ. This handbook is useful for individual use, and it is a resource that any small group ministry can use to train its leaders.

INDIVIDUAL USE

Whether or not your church offers leadership training, you can work through this handbook on your own. In it, you will see why and how you can lead your group members to stay Christ-focused. You will also find valuable suggestions for managing the various challenges that any small group can bring. There are helpful hints on working effectively with a co-leader, connecting with the group members, and handling crisis situations.

Read through each chapter and reflect on the questions asked. If you have a co-leader, we suggest you work through this handbook together.

GROUP TRAINING

To use this book for group training, get a copy of this handbook for all your small group leaders. If you have a group training day, ask each leader or co-leader to read through the chapters and reflect on the included questions ahead of time. Consider your "small group leader training" day as a gathering time for all leaders (new and experienced) to discuss what they've learned from each chapter and to ask questions.

Since participants in small groups might be new Christians, long-time Christians who have never been discipled, or those who have not trusted in Jesus yet, be certain to include training in how to share the gospel and how to disciple young believers in the basics of the Christian faith. This information is included in the RESOURCES section.

What You Will Learn about Being a Christ-Focused Small Group Leader

The following verses are our theme verses for this whole handbook. Read them often. Meditate on them. Memorize them.

> *When I came to you, I did not come with eloquence or human wisdom as I proclaimed to you the testimony about God. For I resolved to know nothing while I was with you except Jesus Christ and him crucified. I came to you in weakness with great fear and trembling. My message and my preaching were not with wise and persuasive words, but with a demonstration of the Spirit's power, so that your faith might not rest on human wisdom, but on God's power. (1 Corinthians 2:1-5)*

Paul knew in his heart and mind that he must stay focused on Christ in his message, manner, and ministry so that all who heard him would rely on Christ first rather than on any human. That is what we are to do as well.

Christ Is Our Focus

Christianity is Christ. It is a relationship with the Lord Jesus Christ. Through the gospel message, Jesus Christ calls you to a new life, clothes you with Himself, commissions you with a purpose to follow Him and make disciples for Him, and empowers you to fulfill that purpose. Small group leaders participate in that commission, pointing women to Christ to meet their needs.

Christ-Like Character

The "Character" chapter covers the role and character qualities of a servant leader in Christ's kingdom. It also includes incorporating one's spiritual gifts and unique behavioral style into a ministry setting.

Christ-Like Commitment

The "Commitment" chapter covers the ongoing commitment to the "nuts and bolts" of small group leadership including commitment to your ministry team and to the women in your group. This includes preparation outside of group time, basic tasks to establish a caring atmosphere for your group meeting, and preparing to manage crisis situations.

Christ-Focused Community

The "Community" chapter covers the importance of making intentional connections to encourage small group participation as well as ways to build and maintain community within a varied group.

Christ-Focused Content

The "Content" chapter emphasizes your authority under Jesus Christ to be the content guardian for your group. You can learn how to maintain Christ-focused content as you direct discussion that will always lead the women to trust in Christ more than on you or the other women in the group.

Christ-Given Commission

The "Commission" chapter covers the role of the small group leader commissioned by Jesus to be a disciple-maker, especially recognizing and coming alongside those who do not know Christ yet or who are new believers.

THE JOY OF SMALL GROUP LEADERSHIP

Being part of a small group can be a most enjoyable experience for a Christ follower. The ideas in this handbook have been developed by those who have spent years being small group leaders. Women of all ages enjoy community and benefit from it when it works well. We pray that you will take to heart these suggestions and become the best Christ-focused small group leader you can be. Enjoy serving Jesus through serving the women in your small group!

Melanie Newton

Christ Is Our Focus

Christianity is Christ!

Christianity **is** Christ. It is not a lifestyle. It's not rules of conduct. It's not a society of people who are joined together by the sprinkling or covering of water. Christianity is a relationship with the Lord Jesus Christ. So before we get to us and our need, let's back up a bit and talk about Jesus.

The New Testament opens with the accounts of Jesus' earthly life recorded in the first 4 books known as the Gospels. Those biblical books called Matthew, Mark, Luke, and John are named after the writer of each account. Each Gospel presents different aspects of Jesus' earthly life and ministry. All present Jesus as "the Christ."

This title "the Christ" is from the Greek word *christos,* a translation of the Hebrew term "Messiah" meaning "anointed one." The Old Testament prophets promised that the Messiah, as the anointed one of God, would come and do many wonderful things for God's people, including a restoration of God's Kingdom on earth. Christians are followers of Jesus, who is the Christ.

UNDERSTANDING THE GOSPEL MESSAGE

The ultimate grace gift came—Jesus Christ. But why did He come? What was His purpose?

From the time sin entered into the relationship of us humans with our Creator God, there is one question that continually demands an answer. "How can any guilty, sinful human be made right in the eyes of a holy God?" Or, in other words, how can God have any kind of a relationship with a sinful human?

We humans have a spiritual problem that can be compared to death caused by a fatal disease. It's a two-fold problem. Sin is the disease. Romans 3:23 says that all have sinned and fallen short of the glory of God. Everyone has the sin disease. And death is the result of the disease. We are born spiritually dead sinners. Our double whammy problem demanded a two-fold solution. The great news is that God acted on our behalf! The gospel is God's cure to that fatal sin disease.

For the problem of sin, people need sin to be removed and replaced with righteousness. *God's answer is Christ's death on the cross.* Because of His finished work on the cross, we can now be cured of the disease.

For the problem of death, people need the restoration of life. *God's answer is Christ's resurrection.* We can now be given life that is forever.

> We suggest you read the blog series, "The Gospel: God's Cure for Our Fatal Sin Disease" on melanienewton.com for more on this topic.

The Gospel message includes the answer to both spiritual problems. A 20th century Bible teacher named Ian Thomas captured the gospel message in a nutshell with these words.

> Jesus Christ **laid down** his life **for** you....so that he could **give** his life **to** you...so that he could **live** his life **through** you. (Ian Thomas, *The Saving Life of Christ*)

The gospel is an announcement to the world of an accomplished fact. What God set out to do for humans, He accomplished. The apostles declared from the time of Pentecost (Acts 2) and beyond that salvation is available on the basis of a single condition. That one condition is faith in Jesus Christ. So it's important to know what faith is and what it is not.

WHAT FAITH IS AND IS NOT

First, let's cover what faith is not. Faith is not a blind belief or mindless gullibility. It is not a life of passivity and doing nothing. Faith is also not a religious feeling like a tingle or good feeling from performing some ritual.

So if faith is not that, what is it? The word "faith" means a "belief, trust, and commitment of mind and heart to something or someone."

- Faith is **intelligent**. That means first you need to know about the something or someone. It is based on information about the object of your faith.

- Faith is also **decisive**. It involves the element of assent or agreement that the information about that someone or something is true.

- Faith **requires an act of the will**. Any conscious choice that involves trust or dependence on someone or something requires a deliberate action to both trust the information and act on it. It is the difference between walking alongside a pool of water (seeing it is there) and floating on the water (experiencing the water personally).

Simply put, faith is a **full commitment to Christ.** God acted. We are to respond to His action by saying yes to faith in Jesus Christ and jumping into the new life God has for us. Instead of believing in your own ability to earn God's favor, you now trust in what Christ has done for you. That's biblical faith.

> *For it is by grace you have been saved, through faith—and this not from yourselves, it is the gift of God—not by works, so that no one can boast. (Ephesians 2:8-9)*

By God's grace, you are saved through your faith. It is by your faith in Jesus alone that you are saved. God offers you salvation from the destruction caused by sin. He offers you this salvation by His grace that is given to you. Grace is an undeserved gift. It is the gift of God—not by works, so that no one can boast of their efforts. Your response is to be one of faith.

Let's say you were standing before God, and He asked you, "Why should I let you into my heaven?" You can answer with confidence, "I know I am saved by your grace through my faith in your Son Jesus Christ." You are in!

So if you have heard the good news of the gospel and believed that Jesus is the Christ, the Son of God, who gave Himself for your sins, you have eternal life just by believing in Him as your Savior.

When did you make that decision to put your faith in Jesus Christ for your salvation?

Jesus is not only your Savior, He is also your Lord—the one who sits at the right hand of His Father God as head over everything else in heaven and on earth. As Lord, Jesus Christ is your *master*—the one to whom you should willingly give your obedience. As Lord, He is your *model* of how to live as a human in a dependent relationship with God. And, as

Lord, He is your *mentor* in walking with you in that dependent relationship.

FOLLOWING CHRIST AS LORD OF YOUR LIFE

Through the gospel message, Jesus Christ calls you to a new life, clothes you with Himself, commissions you with a purpose, and empowers you to fulfill that purpose. Did you know that?

Jesus Christ calls you to a new life.

You get this new life the moment that you put your faith in Him. And it is a life of adventure with Him. The adventure is not only having His life in you but also letting Him live His life through you. The Bible describes that relationship like this,

> *I have been crucified with Christ and I no longer live, but Christ lives in me. The life I live in the body, I live by faith in the Son of God, who loved me and gave himself for me. (Galatians 2:20)*

What an adventure!

Jesus Christ clothes you with Himself.

That beautiful picture is also described in Galatians.

> *So in Christ Jesus you are all children of God through faith, for all of you who were baptized into Christ have clothed yourselves with Christ. (Galatians 3:26-27)*

Everyone who trusts in Christ is identified with Christ, and by that very act, is clothed with Christ. God sees Jesus when He looks on you. You are "in Him." That is your new identity. You become the walking, talking, visible representative of the invisible God.

Jesus Christ commissions you with a purpose.

Before returning to heaven after His resurrection, Jesus said to His followers:

> *All authority in heaven and on earth has been given to Me. Therefore go and MAKE DISCIPLES of all nations, baptizing them in the name of the Father and of the Son and of the Holy Spirit, and teaching them to obey everything I have commanded you. (Matthew 28:18-19)*

This is the commission to all believers. Actually, Jesus commissions you with a two-fold purpose. First, you are to follow Him as His disciple. In John 12:26, Jesus said, "Whoever serves me must follow me." A disciple is an active follower or learner. To follow Jesus as His disciple means that you make the choice to learn from Jesus through what is taught in the Bible and apply those teachings to your life in dependent obedience to Him. That's what you do to grow as a Christian.

Even more than that, you are commissioned to live for Him as a disciple-maker. That sounds scary, but it isn't. A disciple-maker simply reaches others for Christ, builds them up in the faith, and helps them reach their friends for Christ.

When Jesus gave that commission to His followers to go and make disciples, it was not to ordained preachers, hired church staff, or mission organizations. He spoke those words to ordinary, everyday kind of people like you and I are.

That's what small group leaders do. We participate in the commission that Jesus gave to all His followers to be disciples and disciple-makers as we let Him live His life through us. Small groups are great fishing pools for fulfilling this purpose. You, as a small group leader, have the opportunity to pursue disciple-making as you minister to the women of your small group, and you can encourage them to become disciple-makers as well. We'll discuss this more in Chapter 6, "Christ-Given Commission."

Jesus Christ empowers you to fulfill that purpose.

But wait! Our Lord doesn't leave us on our own to do that disciple-making stuff in our lives. He gives His life to us in a powerful way.

> *But you will receive power when the Holy Spirit comes on you; and you will be my witnesses... (Acts 1:8)*
> *Now to him who is able to do immeasurably more than all we ask or imagine, according to his power that is at work within us, (Ephesians 3:20)*

Jesus empowers us through the Holy Spirit present in our lives. Our response is to live dependently on His power by faith.

We can be small group leaders not because we are great or smart and not because we have been a Christian for a long time or know the Bible well. Who makes us able to do what He asks us to do? Jesus does! We are simply to obey Him and trust His Spirit in us to work through us.

How have you helped others to know Jesus and follow Him?

STAYING FOCUSED ON CHRIST

The following verses are our theme verses for this whole handbook. Read them often. Meditate on them. Memorize them.

> *When I came to you, I did not come with eloquence or human wisdom as I proclaimed to you the testimony about God. For I resolved to know nothing while I was with you except Jesus Christ and him crucified. I came to you in weakness with great fear and trembling. My message and my preaching were not with wise and persuasive words, but with a demonstration of the Spirit's power, so that your faith might not rest on human wisdom, but on God's power. (1 Corinthians 2:1-5)*

As Paul traveled to every town to teach, his focus and message was on Christ, not himself. The phrase "fear and trembling" represented humility. His weakness was not a failure, but it was a decision to rely on Christ and His strength rather than on his own. Paul took to heart Jesus's words in John 15:5, "Apart from Me you can do nothing."

Take the pressure off of yourself regarding what you think are expectations of you. Small group leaders will not be perfect. And you are not to be a substitute for the Lord to your group members. You are not responsible to "fix" them. Rather, you are to be an example to them of how to depend on the Lord for everything—how to rely on Him in every area of strength, weakness, and in-between. Point them to Jesus.

The Christian life is one of faith and dependence on Christ. If you are a bit nervous about leading a small group, great! That means you will rely on Him more than on yourself. You are exactly in God's will for you right now.

Human parents raise their children to be less dependent on them and more independent of them. But God raises His children to be **more dependent on Him** and **less independent of Him**. Anything that causes you to rely on Him more is good for you. And that will certainly be true when it comes to leading a small group.

As you embark on this adventure of being a small group leader, remember that you are not alone. Christ is with you every step of the way. He loves those people in your group even more than you could ever love them. He knows their needs. He knows how best to meet those needs. He can do far more than we ask or imagine as He works in us and for us (Ephesians 3:20). Trust Him. It's okay to say to Him at any time, "Lord, I can't, but you can in me." Then, watch what He does! **Christianity is Christ!**

Christ with me, Christ before me, Christ behind me,
Christ in me, Christ beneath me, Christ above me,
Christ on my right, Christ on my left,
Christ when I lie down, Christ when I sit down, Christ when I rise,
Christ in the heart of everyone who thinks of me,
Christ in the mouth of everyone who speaks of me,
Christ in the eye that sees me,
Christ in the ear that hears me.
(From the prayer attributed to the *Confession* by St. Patrick)

Prayer: Ask Jesus to show you how to use your strengths to glorify Him more than yourself. Ask Him to work through your strengths and your weaknesses. Rely on Him to show the women in your group that being dependent on the Lord will make them more effective in living life God's way than they could ever accomplish on their own.

Christ-Like Character

2

The character of a servant-leader

They devoted themselves to the apostles' teaching and to fellowship, to the breaking of bread and to prayer. Everyone was filled with awe at the many wonders and signs performed by the apostles. All the believers were together and had everything in common. They sold property and possessions to give to anyone who had need. Every day they continued to meet together in the temple courts. They broke bread in their homes and ate together with glad and sincere hearts, praising God and enjoying the favor of all the people. And the Lord added to their number daily those who were being saved. (Acts 2:42-47)

Those verses describe the Christian life applied in a small group setting—house churches meeting in Jerusalem led by the apostles. What each of those leaders brought to their small groups was their faith in Jesus Christ, their character, and the way they were uniquely gifted. Likewise, every small group leader in Christ's Church brings to their small group those same things—faith, character, and uniqueness.

Character is defined as "the mental and moral qualities distinctive to an individual." The health of the small group is no doubt impacted by the character of the person leading it. Your character springs from your faith walk with Jesus Christ and is expressed through your unique giftedness.

Think back on your own experiences in a small group. Consider some of your favorite leaders. What character qualities did they have that contributed to an enjoyable group experience?

BEING A CHRIST-FOCUSED LEADER

You have accepted the call to be a small group leader. Yes, this brings responsibility with it. But remember you are not alone. You have Jesus Christ with you. He is plenty big enough to lead you and help you to lead others.

The key to being a Christ-focused leader is for you to be Christ-focused yourself. What does that mean? It means that you make the daily choice for Him to be Lord of your own life. Doing that naturally leads you to follow Him as His disciple and to let Him live His life through you.

As a small group leader, you are acting "in the name of the Lord." That means you are moving under the commission of and according to the character of the one you serve—Jesus Christ. You are under Christ's authority to lead your small group. You are also with authority to serve others in His name. You do so by relying on Him more than on yourself. Others will notice and respond.

> In 1 Corinthians 11:1, Paul said, "Follow my example, as I follow the example of Christ." Paul knew we all need a role model, a picture of Christ that makes the heart, mind, and ways of Christ visible and tangible. To step into a role of leadership is essentially to state, "Follow me as I follow Christ." If people are going to follow us, our primary task is to lead ourselves well ... The first step toward leading yourself well is following well ... And if you are a Christ follower, the practice of following [Christ] well is fundamental to your identity and may be one of the greatest tests of your character. (Heather Zempel, *Community Is Messy*, pp. 67-68)

That's what you bring to your small group. You bring your own relationship with the Lord Jesus Christ. Follow Him well so they can see how to follow Him well. You may have heard it said, "Your walk should match your talk." But that's only true if your talk matches God's talk. One is self-focused (yours); the other is Christ-focused (God's). **Your walk should match God's talk.**

As a small group leader, you are to point the women to Jesus, encouraging them in their relationship with Him above all else. Your goal is to help them learn to place their dependence more upon Christ and less upon you as their leader.

BEING A SERVANT-LEADER

A Christ-focused leader is also a servant-leader. What does that mean? Well, Jesus Himself gave the description for us. He contrasted the world's concept of leader with what He wanted for His Church.

> *Jesus called them (the disciples) together and said, "You know that those who are regarded as rulers of the Gentiles lord it over them, and their high officials exercise authority over them. Not so with you. Instead, whoever wants to become great among you must be your servant, and whoever wants to be first must be slave of all. For even the Son of Man did not come to be served, but to serve, and to give his life as a ransom for many." (Mark 10:42-45)*

Leaders in Christ's Church (elders, deacons, ministry directors, and small group leaders) are to be servant-minded. The phrase "servant-leader" describes this role and heart attitude. A servant-leader considers what is best for those in her group and makes it her goal to serve them according to their needs.

Describe a servant-leader you have known. What made you think of that person?

Several Bible passages describe character qualities of servant leaders. Some are particularly addressed to women. Please read each passage below and the associated character descriptions. We'll begin with our theme verses.

Humility and teachability

> *When I came to you, I did not come with eloquence or human wisdom as I proclaimed to you the testimony about God. For I resolved to know nothing while I was with you except Jesus Christ and him crucified. I came to you in weakness with great fear and trembling. My message and my preaching were not with wise and persuasive words, but with a demonstration of the Spirit's power, so that your faith might not rest on human wisdom, but on God's power. (1 Corinthians 2:1-5)*

The fruit of being Christ-focused is to be humble and teachable.

- **Humility** is a decision you make to recognize God's authority over you and to desire what He wants more than what you want. You know that you've made that decision when you are willing to trust in God's goodness and accept His dealings with you as good without fighting Him on it. Humility is also being vulnerable and sharing your own struggles with your group.

- **Teachability** flows out of humility. It means that you are willing to learn with a humble heart and to submit to God's truth. Women have the freedom in Christ to receive instruction and learn the truths essential to the Christian faith and how to live them out in godliness. God loves it when we are teachable.

You don't need to know all the answers, but you do need to be committed to your own faith walk with Jesus—living by faith and dependence on Him. Notice that Paul's message and preaching were entirely focused on God's Word and His power rather than on Paul's own eloquence or wisdom.

Why would humility be an important quality in a small group leader?

Are you teachable? Would others consider you teachable?

Loving sacrificially

A new command I give you: Love one another. As I have loved you, so you must love one another. By this everyone will know that you are my disciples, if you love one another. (John 13:34-35)

Jesus said this right after He demonstrated sacrificial love for His disciples by washing their feet as a household servant would normally do. He calls every one of His followers to demonstrate sacrificial love towards others. A servant-leader commits to love the women in her group as well as those on her ministry team as Jesus has loved her.

Why would sacrificial love be an important quality in a small group leader?

Respectable, disciplined, and trustworthy

Paul outlines the qualifications for the office of "deacon" in 1 Timothy 3:8-13. Verse 11 particularly addresses women (the Greek term *gune* denotes a woman, whether married or unmarried).

The term deacon (from the Greek meaning "servant") is used in the New Testament for both men and women, although this is not always clear in many English translations. The early church had both male and female deacons who were servant-leaders in their churches.

In the same way, the women are to be worthy of respect, not malicious talkers but temperate and trustworthy in everything." (1 Timothy 3:11)

- **Respectable:** A woman worthy of respect willingly submits to the authority structures in her life, including the authority of Scripture. She strives to live a life worthy of her calling as she considers the well-being of others. Those who know her best recognize this in her.

- **Disciplined in speech and behavior:** Women in leadership must guard the confidences shared within her small group setting or ministry team. She must keep in mind how her words may affect others and be careful not to share sensitive information (personal and/or confidential) in inappropriate settings (with those who don't need to know that information). Use discretion when dealing with ministry concerns by only talking with those directly responsible for the solution.

  Although some associate the word "temperate" with abstaining from alcohol, it really means to be self-controlled. A temperate woman yields to the Holy Spirit's control of her behavior, attitude, and emotions. She chooses unity over personal preference so is known as one who is cooperative and more interested in the goals of the ministry than her own.

- **Trustworthy:** When you are worthy of respect and disciplined in speech and behavior, others know you are trustworthy. This means that you are faithful as Jesus describes it, "faithful in the little things." The oversight and teaching of the church are to be entrusted to those who have proven themselves to be faithful. Leaders are held to a greater accountability. Therefore, we must be diligent in pursuing and abiding in biblical truth.

Why would these be important qualities for a small group leader to have?

Able to teach and model what is good

Likewise, teach the older women to be reverent in the way they live, not to be slanderers or addicted to much wine, but to teach what is good. Then they can urge the younger women to love their husbands and children, to be self-controlled and pure, to be busy at home, to be kind, and to be subject to their husbands, so that no one will malign the word of God. (Titus 2:3-5)

The term "older" can refer to age or spiritual maturity. Mentoring is someone older in the Lord helping someone younger in the Lord understand and apply biblical truth to everyday life.

- **Reverent:** Don't let this term scare you. The Greek word translated "reverent" referred to the work of a priestess serving in the temple of her God. The Bible says that our bodies are a temple of the Holy Spirit. For us as Christ's women, all that we do can be done "as unto the Lord." Our daily life in all its aspects is continual ministry before God as we serve and represent Him before others.

- **Able to teach what is good:** This requires knowing what is good to teach. That comes from knowing Jesus Christ and the Scriptures as your source of truth.

- **Urge others:** We want to draw women to God's Word and truth rather than pushing them away from it. Women look to their leaders as role models and examples to follow. No matter where we are in our own personal faith walk with Jesus, they need to see our desire to allow God to change us and grow us in our daily lives and roles as women.

Who modeled the Christian walk of faith for you and how?

DISCOVER AND INVEST YOUR SPIRITUAL GIFTS

You have been gifted by the Holy Spirit to serve the Body of Christ with one or more spiritual gifts. A spiritual gift is a supernatural capacity for service to God in the Body of Christ. All believers receive the same Holy Spirit but individually receive spiritual gifts that differ, according to the will of the Spirit, to be used for the common good.

Although opinions differ on the actual number of spiritual gifts, the Bible clearly indicates a variety of gifts are given. We get this from key passages such as Romans 12, 1 Corinthians 12 and Ephesians 4. Listed below are some of the gifts and how they are beneficial to the Body of Christ, especially the local church body.

The following list of recognized spiritual gifts is adapted from "The Gifts of the Spirit" by Kenneth Boa accessed at bible.org.

- **Administration** (1 Cor. 12:28): The ability to steer a ministry toward the accomplishment of God-given goals and directives by planning, organizing, and implementing what is needed to accomplish the goal including supervising others. A person may have the gift of leadership without the gift of administration.

- **Discernment** (1 Corinthians 12:10): The ability to clearly discern the spirit of truth and the spirit of error (1 John 4:6). With this gift, one can distinguish reality versus counterfeits, the divine versus the demonic, true versus false teaching, and in some cases, spiritual versus carnal motives.

- **Evangelism** (Ephesians 4:11): The ability to be an unusually effective instrument in leading unbelievers to a saving knowledge of Christ. Some with this gift are most effective in personal evangelism, while others may be used by God in group evangelism or cross-cultural evangelism.

- **Exhortation** (Romans 12:8): The ability to motivate others to respond to the truth by providing timely words of counsel, encouragement, and consolation. When this gift is exercised, believers are challenged to stimulate their faith by putting God's truth to the test in their lives.

- **Faith** (1 Corinthians 12:9: The ability to have a vision for what God wants to be done and to confidently believe that it will be accomplished in spite of circumstances and appearances to the contrary. The gift of faith transforms vision into reality.

- **Giving** (Romans 12:8): The ability to contribute material resources with generosity and cheerfulness for the benefit of others and the glory of God. Christians with this spiritual gift need not be wealthy.

- **Helps** (1 Corinthians 12:28): The ability to enhance the effectiveness of the ministry of other members of the body. Some suggest that while the gift of service is more group-oriented, the gift of helps is more person-oriented.

- **Leadership** (Romans 12:8): The ability to discern God's purpose for a group, set and communicate appropriate goals, and motivate others to work together to fulfill them in the service of God. A person with this gift is effective at delegating tasks to followers without manipulation or coercion.

- **Mercy** (Romans 12:8): The ability to deeply empathize and engage in compassionate acts on behalf of people who are suffering physical, mental, or emotional distress. Those with this gift manifest concern and kindness to people who are often overlooked.

- **Service** (Romans 12:7): The ability to identify and care for the physical needs of the body through a variety of means.

- **Shepherd or pastor** (Ephesians 4:11): A person with this spiritual gift has the ability to personally lead, nourish, protect, and care for the needs of a group of believers. Many with this gift do not have or need the office of pastor to be useful to the body.

- **Teaching** (Romans 12:7; 1 Corinthians 12:28-29; Ephesians 4:11): The ability to clearly explain and effectively apply the truths of God's Word so that others will learn. This requires the capacity to accurately interpret Scripture, engage in necessary research, and organize the results in a way that is easily communicated.

- **Wisdom** (1 Corinthians 12:8): The ability to apply the principles of the Word of God in a practical way to specific situations and to recommend the best course of action at the best time. The exercise of this gift skillfully distills insight and discernment into excellent advice.

Various spiritual gift assessments are available to further help you understand how you have been gifted. We recommend the online spiritual gifts analysis provided by "Ephesians Four Ministries" of the Church Growth Institute at the following website: gifts.churchgrowth.org. Choose the free individual survey.

Please take this assessment (or any other assessment you have available to you). Be sure to allow yourself at least 15 minutes to answer the questions for this analysis. At the end, you will receive a detailed description of what may be your main spiritual gift. Often, a second gift is evident, and that description will be displayed as well. If possible, print these descriptions for future reference.

Primary gift: _____

Secondary gift (if applicable): _____

What did you discover about yourself regarding your spiritual gift(s) and how they could benefit your ministry as a small group leader?

DISCOVER AND INVEST YOUR UNIQUE DESIGN

The health of a small group is impacted by your character flowing from your faith in Christ. And that character is expressed through your unique giftedness. That includes the spiritual gifts God gave you as a believer and how He made you as a unique person. You are uniquely designed in your behavior and innate abilities.

Have you ever asked yourself why you act the way you do? Or, do you wonder why another person reacts the way they do? What you are really observing is human behavior, something that people have been doing since ancient times. Behavior is how you naturally tend to react to the environment around you. This affects how you communicate with others and also how you receive their communication. Behavior is not personality, which is a complex issue usually falling under the realm of psychology. Personality is like tree roots—unseen but developed long before the tree grew tall. Behavior is the visible part of the tree—the trunk and branches.

When God created Adam and Eve, He placed in them genes that would give variety to the human race in hair color, eye color, body shape, size, and also in behavior. Since God made Adam and Eve to complement one another, we can assume they were different in their behavioral tendencies. But together they made a team.

One behavioral strength is not better than another. Some are just more suited to specific tasks. All are needed in a society and definitely in the body of Christ. The main value of recognizing behavioral strengths and weaknesses is to help you understand yourself better as well as those closest to you. You become more aware of what you bring to your ministry team and to your small group.

As the Spirit works to conform us to the image of Christ, He opens our eyes to recognize our need for Him. In our strengths and weaknesses and everywhere in-between, the challenge for us is to let God grow us in our areas of weakness and to appreciate others who are strong in the areas where we are weak.

One behavioral assessment tool that is often used in ministry settings is called the "DISC Dimensions of Behavior" or DISC for short. It comes in many different forms with varied names for the categories. But the DISC helps you to understand yourself better, recognize and develop your strengths, and develop teamwork with your co-leader or ministry partners.

The DISC recognizes four basic categories (or, dimensions) of behavior based upon whether one is:

- fast-paced or slow-paced in reacting to one's environment
- task-oriented or people-oriented by nature

Examine the diagram below. Mark where you think you fit.

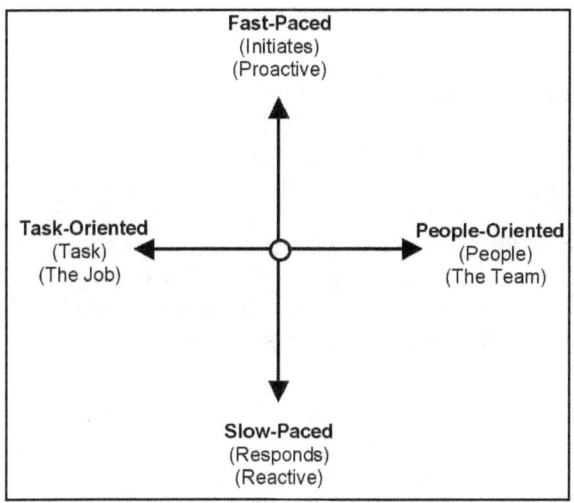

For better understanding, go to www.123test.com/disc-personality-test to take the free DISC assessment online. Focus on how you behave in a specific environment such as your home or ministry. This is not a test—no "right" or "wrong" answers, no "pass" or "fail." Go with your first impressions, and do this from your point of view, not what another person would say about you. The goal is to give you information to help you become more aware of yourself and others. If nothing seems to match "you," retake the assessment.

Once you complete the assessment, write your primary and secondary tendencies below.

Primary behavioral tendency _____

Secondary behavioral tendency (if applicable) _____

Read the description of each behavioral tendency in the RESOURCES section of this book. You can use this information to enable you to communicate and work well with others so as to encourage them to reach their potential as well.

What enlightened you about yourself as you read the results of the DISC assessment?

STAYING FOCUSED ON CHRIST

Staying focused on Christ means that you recognize your need for Christ in every area of your life. You give to Him all the skills, talents, advantages, and opportunities He has given you and then use them for His glory. Sometimes, our strengths can be our greatest hindrances. We tend to rely on that rather than on God. So relying on God means submitting your strengths and your weaknesses to Him for His purposes in your life and in how you lead your small group.

Having Christ-like character means that you choose to be a God-dependent woman—not "independent except for when you need Him." But you choose to be God-dependent all that time. Being God-dependent is not weakness. It is being stronger and having more influence, success, and satisfaction than you could ever have through your own efforts—as brilliant and self-sufficient as you think you are or as weak and messed up as you think you are and everywhere in-between.

Staying focused on Christ should lead you to celebrate your unique design and giftedness by bringing Him glory as you use your gifts in the Body of Christ.

You can have confidence in what the Lord Jesus Christ will do in your life so that you will want to depend on Him more than on yourself. As you submit to Him, our God will transform you into a God-dependent woman who lives dependently on Him in weakness and in strength. Your small group will benefit from this.

> *Prayer:* Ask Jesus to help you recognize your need for Him in every area of your life. Give to Him all that He has given to you in your unique design and spiritual gifts. Ask Him to use those in your life to draw the women in your group to Christ.

Christ-Like Commitment

The commitment of leadership

A commitment is "a devotion or dedication to a cause, person, or relationship." As a small group leader, you are making a commitment both to your group and to the ministry as a whole. What does that look like? What is involved in the day-to-day, ongoing management of a small group?

COMMITMENT TO THE GREATER MINISTRY

As part of a ministry team

Let us consider how we may spur one another on toward love and good deeds. (Hebrews 10:24)

Every small group leader is part of the greater ministry of either a local body of believers or the universal Body of Christ in general. No one is alone. Jesus not only gathered together His group of apostles, He taught them how to work together to carry on the ministry after His earthly departure. The Holy Spirit is given to every believer to equip each one with gifts needed to grow Christ's kingdom on earth.

We were never intended to work alone but in connection with others who have a faith walk with Jesus Christ. A connection is "a relationship in which one person is linked or associated with another person." Ministry leaders need to pursue love for and connection with one another to share the burdens and joys of ministry as well as to support and encourage one another in the use of one's gifts.

If you have leaders' meetings or ministry planning meetings, make it a priority for you to attend those so you are better prepared to lead an effective discussion with your group or to stay informed about anything that might affect your group.

Staying united through agreement guidelines

For many small group ministries, the leaders generally come from various church backgrounds. Each small group leader is also learning and growing in her faith walk with Jesus. It's important to your ministry that you are supporting one another in the most important doctrines of the Christian faith.

Your ministry probably has a statement of faith associated with it. Some parts of that statement may be considered "non-negotiable," that is, all leaders are expected to not only agree with those doctrines but also support those positions should they come up in small group. Some examples of non-negotiable doctrines might be:

- The Bible is the inspired Word of God.
- God is a Trinity: three persons in one.
- Jesus is God, not just a human religious teacher.
- Jesus died and rose from the grave for the sins of the world.
- The Holy Spirit is God and not just a force or an energy.
- Salvation is by grace alone through faith, apart from works.
- All believers, once saved, are eternally secure in Christ.

We suggest you get a copy of your ministry's "Statement of Faith," read through it, and make note of anything you need to clarify or discuss further with your ministry team leader.

What are the "Non- Negotiable Doctrines" for your group?

Is there anything in your group's Statement of Faith with which you don't fully agree or about which you have further questions?

Based on the list you wrote above, is it a non-negotiable?

- **No:** It is not on the non-negotiable list. It's probably okay for you to not intellectually hold the same position as your ministry on those. But be sure to ask your questions to your ministry director for your own growth.
- **Yes:** It is on the non-negotiable list. Please make an appointment with your ministry team leader to discuss that issue.

If you do not agree with a "non-negotiable" doctrine, your ministry leadership needs to know this. You may be asked to verbally support the ministry position or refrain from discussion. If you cannot defend the ministry's position, you can choose to direct someone to the proper authority who can explain that position.

WORKING WITH A CO-LEADER OR VOLUNTEER ASSISTANT

Every small group needs someone who can manage the discussion and the time plus someone who can build relationships and nurture the group. Rarely is one person gifted to do both. It helps if your ministry is set up to have co-leaders for every group that complement each other. If you do not have a co-leader, ask the Lord Jesus to show you a mature woman in your group that can help you manage some of the tasks that you will have difficulty doing alone. When you trust this to Him, He will help you. That's being Christ-focused.

What do you think might be a struggle for you as a small group leader? For example: time use, follow-up, leading a discussion, consistent attendance, etc.

What will you need your co-leader or someone from your group to help you do in those areas?

If you have a co-leader...

Talk with your co-leader about your group on a regular basis. You are a team with different perspectives and unique observations and ideas. Work together for your combined "best."

Consider how to best use your behavioral strengths and weaknesses as well as your spiritual gifts to minister to the group.

> **Ask each other:** What is your natural bent in leadership? Do you like to lead the discussion? Do you like to write notes, e-mail, or call the group members? Do you like to spend time getting to know the women in your group one-on-one? Will you share those responsibilities or divide them up?

Some group leaders like to alternate leading the discussion. Others prefer to let one lead the discussion while the other does the follow-up with the group members. What will you do?

Talk about how to regularly connect with your small group members. Which one of you will do this and how?

Decide how often you will talk about the group and pray together for the women in your group. If a group member shares a prayer request or a prayer need comes up, make sure that you both know that and will remember to pray for that woman's need and follow up with her. Pray for each other regularly.

Consider what to do if you are going to be absent from your small group meeting. Who needs to know and how soon? Will someone need to substitute for you in group time?

> *Have you had a co-leader in another group? How did you connect with her effectively? What did you do to work together using each other's strengths in the best way for the group?*

If you don't have a co-leader...

Ask the Lord Jesus to help you identify a woman in your group to help you in ministry to your group members. Look for someone who already demonstrates some spiritual maturity and commitment to your group. She might in the future be invited to become a small group leader herself. You, in essence, help her develop as a leader who is capable of ministering to others.

Give her that responsibility within the group and watch what she does. Pray for her regularly. Enjoy your new relationship and leave the results up to the Holy Spirit!

MANAGE CONFLICTS AND UNMET EXPECTATIONS

Conflict between women in ministry happens. The key is to manage it in a godly way. See examples of that in the following scriptures.

> *I appeal to you, ... in the name of our Lord Jesus Christ, that all of you agree with one another so that there may be no divisions among you and that you may be perfectly united in mind and thought. (I Corinthians 1:10)*

> *Do nothing out of selfish ambition or vain conceit, but in humility consider others better than yourselves. (Philippians 2:3)*

Unity or like-mindedness with your ministry team is essential for a servant-leader of a small group. But conflicts will naturally arise between women who have different behavioral tendencies, backgrounds, and/ or approaches to ministry. We must all work hard to resolve conflicts quickly for the health of the ministry.

Conflicts usually fall into 2 categories:

1) Conflict with the ministry operation
2) Conflict with a ministry co-leader

Some examples of potential conflicts are: behavioral clashes, how one does/does not nurture the group, childcare issues, doctrinal issues, and/ or misunderstanding of ministry directives. We've given you some suggestions for resolving behavioral clashes using "The DISC Dimensions of Behavior" in the RESOURCES section at the end of this book. We offer more suggestions below.

Conflict regarding the ministry operation

We recommend that you bring any issues or concerns to the coordinator or staff member that oversees your ministry. Ask questions and listen well. This will hopefully give you a new perspective on why your leaders do things the way they do. This should also give you an avenue for your concern or idea to be discussed and considered for the benefit of the entire group.

Conflict with another ministry leader

Assume good will on her part and ask the Lord how best to proceed in your relationship with her. If you need to discuss the issue in order to get guidance on how to proceed, set aside some time to talk with your ministry leader. Do not gossip about the situation with others. When needed, talk directly with the other leader for the purpose of reconciliation. See Matthew 18:15-17 for a good passage on dealing with conflict biblically.

Christ-focused unity

Working together as a ministry team (leader/co-leader for each group and leaders in the ministry) benefits all the participants in the ministry. And our Lord Jesus is glorified by our unity. This is evident in His prayer for us:

> *My prayer is not for them alone. I pray also for those who will believe in me through their message, that all of them may be one, Father, just as you are in me and I am in you. May they also be in us so that the world may believe that you have sent me. I have given them the glory that you gave me, that **they may be one as we are one**: I in them and you in me. May they be brought to **complete unity** to let the world know that you sent me and have loved them even as you have loved me. (John 17:20-23)*

> **Have you had a co-leader that didn't do her part in caring for the group? Or have you had one that lacked the Christian maturity needed for the group? How did you handle that?**

> **Have you experienced or witnessed a conflict between women in ministry? How was it managed or resolved? What, if anything, could have been done better?**

COMMITMENT TO YOUR SMALL GROUP

Some responsibilities of a small group leader are considered the "nuts and bolts" of your commitment. Paying attention to these will help you be an effective servant-leader to the members of your group. Having a co-leader or volunteer assistant will make it easier.

#1 Prepare ahead to serve your group.

Preparing ahead to serve your group means that you are **committed to spending time with Jesus and His Word yourself**. As you rely on Him, you are better prepared to be a Christ-focused leader for your group. It also means that you will consistently pray for each of the women in your group. And you will commit to pray for yourself as leader and for your group time to stay focused on Christ.

When you take the time to prepare before your group meeting, this **frees you to focus on the women during your group time** and not be distracted by other tasks. This may take the form of reviewing the Bible Study lesson or the discussion topic and planning how to direct the discussion. If someone else is leading the discussion, you still need to be prepared to support her during that time. Glance at the next lesson before going to your group. This allows you to offer suggestions to your ladies on difficult questions as they prepare for the next week.

Review the burdens or struggles your women are facing so that you can encourage them or ask for follow-up in a discreet way.

Arrive early enough to set up the room and anything else before any of the women arrive. If you don't have any set up to do, get yourself settled in the room before any of your group members normally arrive so that you are ready to greet them. Being there on time, even early, sends a positive and welcoming message to each woman in the group.

Sit so you can face the entrance to the room. Whenever someone comes, you can quickly give a welcoming smile and even a wave to let them know you are happy to see them. This simple planned positioning helps to establish a caring atmosphere.

What will be your biggest challenge in preparing beforehand to serve your group?

#2 Manage time wisely.

You and your co-leader (if you have one) need to ensure that group time is used wisely, not only for small group discussion but also for caring for one another.

Start your small group on time, at least by 5 minutes after the official time, even if only a few women are present. Doing this will honor those who arrive on time. And it will encourage the rest to be prompt as well.

If you are not leading the discussion, learn to help your co-leader move the group along. Watch the time and any signals given by the leader. Graciously interrupt a discussion when needed by saying, *"We had better move along, or we won't finish (get to the part you really want to discuss)."*

Do your best to end on time. Plan to stop and pray before the official end time and do so even if you aren't finished covering the day's lesson.

Consider what you will do if something happens that totally interrupts your time (for example, a woman breaks down in tears). See Chapter 4: "Christ-Focused Community" for ideas.

> *Why is it important to manage group time wisely? Will this be a challenge for you?*

#3 Prepare to manage crisis situations.

Things can happen unexpectedly—bad weather, an injury, sudden illness, or even a potentially dangerous situation. Instead of wondering what to do when it happens, prepare yourself with some basic bits of information to manage most crisis situations, such as your meeting location address and where to find safe areas. If you are meeting in a church building, find out your church's plans for all of these.

> *See "Group Meeting Location Details" in the RESOURCES section. Fill out the needed information about your meeting location.*

Below are some suggestions to help you manage various crisis situations:

- **Sudden illness or accident within your group:** In the case of an obvious medical emergency (symptoms of heart attack or stroke, unconsciousness, severe bleeding), call 911. Ask the Lord to help you to remain calm and for the person to be protected. Do not attempt to handle anything other than normal first aid responses while awaiting emergency services (unless you are a trained medical professional). Also, contact your ministry director or a church staff member, if applicable.

- **Fire alarm sounds or a fire is discovered:** If a fire emergency exists, ask the Lord to help you remain calm, which will help your group members to remain calm. Count the number of people in your group. Keep that in mind as you head to the designated evacuation area. Make sure all of your group members are with you. Do not leave your group unattended to obtain first aid. If you are part of a larger ministry, await further instructions from a ministry leader.

- **Extreme weather alert (tornado, damaging winds):** During periods of inclement weather, designate someone to maintain a watch on the current conditions and inform you when to act. Should action need to be taken, ask the Lord to help you remain calm, which will help your group members to remain calm. Count the number of people in your group. Keep that in mind as you head to the shelter area. Upon arrival, count again to insure everyone from your group is with you. Instruct everyone to sit on the floor, back to the wall, hands interlocked covering neck. Do not evacuate the building unless given instruction to do so by an official. Do not leave your group unattended to obtain first aid. Ask for first aid to be brought to you as needed. If you are part of a larger ministry, await further instructions from a ministry leader.

- **Assailant in the building or other security breach:** Ask the Lord to give you calmness as you secure your meeting place. Direct group members to a corner of the room out of sight of the main doorway, close the door, and close any blinds if windows are present. Tables turned sideways can be used as barriers. If in an auditorium, go to a side room. Wait for further instructions from the ministry leader or emergency officials.

What do you need to do to prepare yourself mentally and spiritually for any of the potential crisis situations in this section?

STAYING FOCUSED ON CHRIST

Your commitment to the small group ministry is a faith commitment. You are to do this by faith. Yes, you might feel overwhelmed at what was shared in this chapter. But anything that causes us to rely on Christ more than on ourselves is good for us. That includes being a Christ-focused small group leader.

You are not on your own in this ministry. He will get you through it. And remember that you can at any time say this to Him, "Lord, I can't do this. But you can do this in me and through me. I will trust you." Then, watch what He does!

> **Prayer:** Ask the Lord Jesus to lead you as you commit to being a small group leader. Ask Him to help you team well with your co-leader or volunteer assistant. Pray for yourself to stay Christ-focused as a leader and for your ministry partners to do that as well.

Christ-Focused Community

Building community in a group

Through this handbook, we hope you've gained confidence in what you are bringing to a small group in your character and giftedness. You've made the commitment to your ministry team and to your small group. The next step is to know what to do during group time.

When you are with your group, you have two basic roles:

Role #1. Content Guardian
Role #2. Community Builder

Those two roles are very much interlinked. Yet, if you discuss great content without building community, the group will not gel. So let's focus on building Christ-focused community first. We'll focus on maintaining Christ-focused content in the next chapter.

Several years ago, my friend Joan shared the following scenario at our women's small group leader training. This so aptly describes how many women feel when they attend a small group for the first time.

Imagine with me that you're on a plane to Greece. You've wanted to go there all your life, but you've also been hesitant because you don't know the language or the culture ... AND there is SO much you want to see and do, you don't know where to start!

You're excited, but getting more and more nervous that this was a mistake. What made you think you could travel alone to a foreign country! The plane lands. Where do you go? What if customs won't let you through? What if you can't even find the bathroom?

What if...........wait, there is a smiling face holding a sign with YOUR NAME. You approach the smiling face, and she welcomes you to Greece IN ENGLISH and tells you that your travel agent back home contacted her to help you as you begin your journey. She comfortably navigates you through baggage and customs until you are standing in the beauty of the country you've always wanted to explore. She equips you with local maps, landmark suggestions, historical information, and makes sure you know the words for "bathroom" and "McDonalds hamburger" (in case you need some

American food). You are now free to roam and discover Greece, always KNOWING that your guide, and new friend, is there to help you when needed. Soon, what was unknown becomes familiar. Your trip is a huge success and the experience of a lifetime. And you're eager to return to discover more!!

Ladies, YOU are the smiling face, and YOU can make a difference to women coming to your small group for whatever reason, with whatever anxieties. You can help navigate your women to discover an experience of a lifetime in their walk with God, and to become more familiar with His Word and truth so they are eager to return and discover more!

How many women can walk into almost any room, anytime, and feel comfortable? Your group will have the confident, the nervous, and the insecure. You are that welcoming tour guide...that smiling face...that friend to welcome the women to the community of a small group.

The life of following Christ was never meant to be solitary. The early Christians pursued it in groups not much larger than our small groups. They met exclusively in homes for the first 200 years after the resurrection. By meeting in a small group, we are imitating a time-tested format for spiritual life.

One definition for community is "a feeling of fellowship with others, as a result of sharing common attitudes, interests, and goals." Some of the sharing may include these:

√ Encouraging one another during good and bad times

√ Asking thoughtful questions when one has a decision to make

√ Benefiting from one another's insights into the Word of God

√ Praying for each other

√ Practicing how to love each other

√ Learning to receive care from others

√ Experiencing the joy of watching God work in someone's life

√ Getting to know each other outside of group time

Small groups are the ideal setting in which women can learn what it means to take on the character of Christ. Remembering what you have gained by participating in a small group will help you as a leader.

CONNECTION IS THE FOUNDATION FOR COMMUNITY

As described in the last chapter, connection is a key word for ministry teams to work together—for example, connecting with your co-leader if you have one. But **connection** is also a key word for building community in a group. Connect, connect, connect!

1. Connect the women with YOU.

Picture each woman wearing a sign that says, "Do you care about me?" She wants you to pursue a relationship with her. Through your actions, you say, "I care about you." Here are some ways to connect the women with you.

√ Establish contact by calling each one and welcoming her to the group (even before the first session, if possible). Ask if she has any questions.

√ If they miss the first session, make sure she has her study book or other materials she needs to prepare for the next meeting. Deliver them personally, if necessary. Briefly tell her about the group members since she missed the first day's "Get to Know You" time.

√ Get to know each woman by name and face. Greet them by name whenever you see them.

√ Put their contact information in your phone. Consider taking a picture of each one with your phone.

√ Become familiar with their family member's names and general ages.

√ Pay attention to the needs and hurts expressed by each woman in your group so you can pray for them.

√ Take notice of their skills, interests, and gifts and suggest opportunities for them to be used. For example, if you have a photographer in the group, ask her to take a group photo.

√ Know where your group members live and work, if that seems important to them.

√ Sit by a different woman each meeting and chat with them.

√ Love them through smile, words, and touch. Carefully listen when women share with you, taking notes as needed.

√ Actively seek interaction with them outside of small group.

If you successfully connect her with you, you have a greater chance of her connecting with the other women in the group because she'll want to come.

> The more you get to know a person, the more you get to teach them. (Howard Hendricks)

Has a small group leader intentionally connected with you? How did that influence your desire to attend the group meeting?

2. Connect the women with EACH OTHER.

At the start of a small group, most of the women are strangers. The challenge for the leader is to help this group of strangers get acquainted and become friends who learn to care for one another. It has been said that every woman needs 3 connections to stay in a small group. The connection with you is the first one, also with your co-leader if you have one. They need to connect with at least two more group members. Ask the Lord for ways to build connections in your small group.

√ Be a "matchmaker." Pay attention to common interests (occupations, hometowns or home states, pets, ages of children, live in the same neighborhood, etc.). Encourage those with common interests to get to know one another.

√ When one is absent, let the rest of the group know what is going on and encourage them to join together to pray or help her.

√ Plan for your group to get together outside of normal group time. Even if only 2 can attend, they can connect with one another.

√ Discourage discussing topics that may isolate anyone or divide the group.

√ Other ideas?

Have you seen a small group leader do this well? How did that affect the group?

3. Connect through PRAYING for one another.

One of the best ways to build community and trust among "strangers" is to pray for one another. As the women share their joys and struggles, love grows. That includes you as a leader. Give them insight into your own faith walk with Jesus. This helps them to identify with you as an ordinary woman, not the "superior" leader.

Sharing one another's burdens in prayer helps to build community within the group. It is important to figure out how you will gather the prayer requests from group members and encourage the group to pray for one another. Managing the time and ways to do so is a challenge. Here are a few suggestions:

- √ **Group Journal:** Pass a common prayer journal around the group. When it is time to pray, one woman can read aloud the requests and then pray for them.

- √ **Verbal Requests:** At prayer time, let the women briefly share requests and quick updates on previous requests.

- √ **Individually Written Requests:** Provide slips of paper so that each person can briefly write her prayer need. Put them in a basket for women to pick from and pray for that day and all week. Or, give them all to one person who prays for them during group time then emails them to the group.

- √ **2-3 Together:** Group 2-3 women together to share prayer requests and pray for each other. Change the groups often.

- √ **Private requests:** If anyone wants a prayer request to be seen only by the leader(s), ask her to write "Private" on her request and to fold it in half when she hands it to you. Caution: *Remember not to ask her about the issue in front of other members of the group!*

Reinforce the need to keep confidentiality of what is shared in the group and in the prayer requests of the group members. That encourages trust that builds community.

ENCOURAGING TRUST IN YOU AND ONE ANOTHER

Women join and/or participate in a small group in order to have some need met. As a servant of Jesus Christ and relying upon Him, **it is not your responsibility to meet the needs that only He can meet.** But He has called you into this ministry and gifted you with what you need to serve your group well. As the servant-leader for your group, your role is to make being part of a group "easier" for those who participate. Doing so encourages trust that builds community.

First-time participants will often have underlying questions and concerns about their participation in a small group setting. These are more often **felt** rather than verbalized: *Will I be accepted or rejected here? I'm afraid I'll look stupid or nervous. Will I feel pressured to perform in some way?*

Some other feelings, concerns and fears that women might have when they are meeting with their small group for the first time are these: *Who will be the real leaders here? Will I embarrass myself? How much should I share? What if I'm asked to do something I don't want to do?*

You may have had these same questions in your mind when you joined a small group for the first time. These feelings of awkwardness and anxiety are issues of trust. The person is wondering whom they can really trust in this group. And establishing trust takes time and the ongoing feel of a caring atmosphere. Most women cannot walk into any room, at any time, and instantly feel comfortable. Your group will have the confident, the nervous, and the insecure. You are their "welcoming guide" so they will want to continue their journey week-to-week.

Here are some ways you can help make walking into the group a highlight of a woman's week:

√ Arrive early enough to your group to greet the first woman. We mentioned this in the chapter on commitment.

√ Ensure emotional comfort by asking non-threatening questions such as "How long have you lived here?" or "Tell me a little about yourself." To stay sensitive about personal issues, wait a few sessions before asking about family, children, and marriage.

√ Do not speak in a critical manner about any church, denomination, or political figure. Try to quickly diffuse any such topics when they come up.

√ Communicate unconditional acceptance in your eyes, manner, and the way you respond to what a group member shares. They need to trust you won't make quick judgments about them. They need to be assured of confidences being kept.

What did a past small group leader do to establish a caring atmosphere for your group?

GRACIOUSLY RESPOND TO COMMON CHALLENGES

The complexion of a small group will be as varied as the women attending. Every woman has a need to **feel** heard, a need to **be** valued, a need to **experience** love, and a need to **contribute**. Occasionally, leaders will face some challenging situations emerging from the behavioral tendencies and life situations of the women participants. How we handle these challenges may influence how well our group trusts us as leaders and experiences community. Remember that unstated question, "Who will be the real leader here?"

A leader can help the individual and the group meet these challenges by loving each woman and by redirecting and giving perspective as needed. Ask the Lord to help you understand each person in your group. He knows each woman best. Ask Him to give you gracious ways to handle each challenging situation.

Here are some common challenges brought by individuals to a group and gracious ideas others have discovered for responding to them in a Christlike way.

An overly talkative woman

Managing talkative people graciously is probably the biggest challenge for new small group leaders. For the health of the group, you cannot let them dominate the discussion. But they need to feel valued by the group as much as any other member. So how do you do that?

Most of the time, women know that they talk too much. If you are the talkative one, mark the question(s) where you will share your answers. Otherwise, let the group members answer the questions.

Recognize that some people are just uncomfortable with silence so they feel the need to answer every question. Model to them that you are not uncomfortable with silence, even asking the group to think about their answer for a bit before speaking up.

- **What you can say:** Ask Jesus to give you the words to jump in and sum up what they just said. *Good answer, I appreciate that.* OR *Thank you, _____. (Quickly) Okay, now someone else.* You can also ask Jesus to have another person in the group jump into the discussion graciously.

- **What you can do:** Avoid looking directly at her, which often encourages her to speak. You can also ask her apart from the group, *"What clue do I use to let you know you're talking too much?"* Work out a signal between the two of you when they are talking too much. If you do it graciously, most people will respond just fine.

Keep being gracious about this—firm but gracious. The group depends on you to not let the talkative people take control.

If you've been in a group with an "overly talkative woman," what did the leader do to graciously listen then appropriately move the discussion along?

An excessively shy woman

Shy women will often tell you that they prefer to listen. If they have something to say, they'll say it. You don't have to force opportunity for them to talk. When they do, be sure to listen well and affirm their answer!

- **What you can say:** Ahead of time, *"Do you want me to encourage you to speak up?"* When she does speak, say, *"Thank you, _____, for sharing that insight we all needed."*

- **What you can do:** When she's about to say something, don't let someone else jump into the discussion instead. Call the shy one's name, and ask if she has something to share. Try to offer small groups of 2-4 people to discuss some questions. This helps the quieter ones feel the freedom to share. But don't put her in a group with a dominant talker.

What have you seen a small group leader do to graciously minister to an "excessively shy woman?"

A woman with a chronic illness

This can be frightening because of the potential time demands. Don't try to do it all. We have to balance our care of others with our commitment to our own families. It doesn't matter if you don't know what to do, just "be." Keep a willing heart, stay connected, meet needs, be realistic, and set boundaries.

Here are some ways to realistically and graciously meet needs without overwhelming anyone:

- **What you can say:** *"I have to go to the grocery store. Is there something you need?" "I have just a few minutes but wanted to call and check on you." "I can do that. I'll just need to be home by 3:00 for my kids." "My plate is kind of full today. Can this wait a day or two?"*

- **What you can do:** You can set aside half a day to help with a specific need and let her know. Find out if she needs transportation for medical appointments and take her if you can. Ask if her family needs help with meals on any particular days. Ask what her greatest challenges are, and let the group know about them. Discuss with your co-leader (if you have one) the needs you can help meet, either as a group or individually, or the hurts that you may need to address. Spread the care among the group members as much as you can. Call in assistance from your church when the need overwhelms your group.

What have you seen a small group leader do to graciously minister to a woman with a "chronic illness?"

A woman with intense emotional pain

A little girl was sent on an early errand by her mother, but she took far too much time to return home. When she finally did return, her mother wanted to know what had taken so long. The little girl explained that on the way she had met a little friend who was crying because she had broken her doll. "Oh," said the mother, "then you stopped to help her fix the doll?" "Oh, no," replied the little girl, "I stopped to help her cry."

This little girl knew exactly what her friend needed. When people are hurting, they need comfort. But we often respond to hurting people in unproductive ways. None of us can know the depth of someone's emotional pain. We can only direct them to the reality of our Lord's comfort. And He often uses us to give His comfort to those who are emotionally hurting:

- **What you can say:** *"If you need a shoulder to cry on, use mine."* *"I can't fix it, but I know Who can help. And I'll be here, also."* After a couple of minutes of letting her share and/or cry, say, *"Let's stop and pray for you right now."* Then, do it.

- **What you can do if a woman breaks down in tears in the meeting:** Sensitively listen and pass the Kleenex while at the same time keeping the group from asking more questions that might prolong the sharing. You want to point her to Jesus as much as possible and not let the group try to "fix" her situation. After ~5 minutes, if the woman is still overcome by emotion, the co-leader (or another woman) should **take her aside** to continue giving her support through listening and prayer.

Keep a willing heart, stay connected, meet needs, be realistic and set boundaries. Sometimes her pain may need pastoral counseling or professional help. If that is the case, please direct her to someone in your ministry leadership who can make that evaluation.

What have you seen a small group leader do to graciously minister to someone with "intense emotional pain?"

An argumentative woman

Some women enjoy "stirring the pot" to create a lively debate. Most small groups are not set up for this. Or you may have a woman in your group who says things to be controversial and argumentative. For the sake of the group, you must graciously handle this. Ask the Lord to give you the words to respond or to know whether to let the comment go and move on. We'll discuss this more in Chapter 5: "Christ-Focused Content."

- **What you can say:** *"I understand how you might feel that way." "Can we save that question until later?" "Let's get together and go over that outside of small group." "For years, people have disagreed on that one. We won't be able to solve the mystery* here." "For the purpose of this group, we will follow the faith statement of our ministry."

- **What you can do:** Follow through with what you promised about getting together with her to talk more about her question. If the comment will affect the group because it is a false teaching, gently bring them back to what we can know that is true. Keep loving her and affirming her when she adds good insight to the discussion.

What have you seen a small group leader do to graciously minister to a woman who is "argumentative?"

A woman who attends infrequently

Some women are hesitant at making a commitment to a group. They stay on the fringes of the group through occasionally attending, rarely doing the lesson, or rushing in and out of the meeting. Leaders must do what we can to make them feel welcome and wanted in the group.

Be creative in keeping her connected to the group so that when she does attend, she feels welcomed. You can do that through pursuing a regular connection with her through text, email, or phone call to find out what's going on in her life and to let her know about the group. Continually let her know that she is valued and wanted. Pray for her. Ask the Lord to help you connect with her.

Likewise, keep the group informed about what is going on in her life. It also helps to keep mentioning her name every group gathering so they'll remember her and will not consider her a stranger when she does attend.

What have you seen a small group leader do to graciously minister to a woman who "attends infrequently?"

A woman new to the Bible

Small groups attract new Christians as well as those who have been believers for years but have never been discipled. Even non-Christians are attracted to small groups because they are seeking truth and/or fellowship. This is true for Bible studies, mothers' groups, or other small groups. A small group is a great opportunity to help someone grow in their relationship with Jesus and in His truth.

- **Acknowledge her presence:** If your small group is a Bible study, assume that some of the women might not know how to find a Bible verse, read it, and answer a question. Pay attention to what she shares about herself. Some leaders ask right away if this is anyone's first Bible study.

- **Sympathize with her insecurity:** Come alongside her and let her know you want to help her as much as you can. Encourage her to ask questions. Communicate with your face and your words that you are happy to have her in the group. Encourage the other group members to be gracious to her.

- **Provide the best tutoring:** Offer to meet with her outside of group time to work through a few lessons. Tell her that the Lord wants her to understand His Word so He will help her to do so. Make sure she has a Bible or Bible app. Show her how to use it.

- **Be prepared to share the gospel with a non-Christian:** Every woman's greatest need is to know Jesus Christ as her Savior. See Chapter Six "Christ-Given Commission" for ways to share the gospel with someone who doesn't know Jesus yet and then disciple her as a new Christian.

Get more information on this topic at melanienewton.com. Search "Nurture Women New to the Bible." Watching someone discover the riches of God's Word and a relationship with Christ is infectious to the rest of the group. It's a win/win!

When group members drop out

You may be tempted to take it personally when women drop out of your group—whether they tell you they are dropping, or they just stop coming. You might start wondering what you did wrong. Insecurity creeps in which can certainly affect your confidence. Some people sign up for a Bible study group with good intentions of doing the lessons and attending regularly. But life gets in the way. Give that to Jesus!

It's okay to try to find out the reasons why they drop out without being defensive or suspicious. More than likely, it's not your leadership but that person's season of life. Or, their schedule has changed preventing them from continuing.

Be proactive about connecting with newcomers especially. If you intentionally connect with someone who stays on the "fringe" or the outside of the group, there is a higher likelihood that they will continue to try out the group. Then, you have a better chance to connect her with the other group members.

A shrinking group size can also be discouraging to the other members. Continue working on building community with the faithful attendees and focus on Christ and His purpose for those that remain.

If the group size is getting noticeably smaller as members drop out, how would you keep the rest of the members from getting discouraged?

STAYING FOCUSED ON CHRIST

Be shepherds of God's flock that is under your care, watching over them—not because you must, but because you are willing, as God wants you to be; not pursuing dishonest gain, but eager to serve; not lording it over those entrusted to you, but being examples to the flock. (1 Peter 5:2-3)

Care, wisdom, and discernment are needed in shepherding the women God sends to your group. Your role as community builder is to encourage Christ-focused community in your group. You do this through connection, turning to the Lord in prayer, loving each other with patience and understanding, and fostering a safe environment of trust and confidentiality.

Jesus Christ sent the women to your group and loves them very much. He knows their hearts. He knows their needs. He knows you and the gifts He has given to you. He wants you to rely on Him to shepherd the women in your group well.

Prayer: Ask the Lord Jesus for wisdom in how to manage the marvelously varied women in your group. Ask Him to build community among them that is focused on Him more than on you. Ask Jesus to help you respond graciously to any challenge. Depend on Him to show you what to do. He is faithful! Pray for yourself to stay Christ-focused and Christ-dependent as a leader.

Christ-Focused Content

The authority of a content guardian

As we mentioned in the previous chapter, you have two basic roles when you are meeting with your group:

Role #1. Content Guardian
Role #2. Community Builder

Those two roles are very much interlinked. If you discuss great content without building community, the group will not gel. Yet, while the group community is getting established, the members depend upon you to make sure the content of the discussion stays on track and is fruitful. So in this chapter, we'll focus on how you, as a content guardian, can maintain Christ-focused content.

A guardian is a "custodian, a keeper, or someone who maintains control of something important." For a Bible study, the "something important" is the truth from God's Word and handling it correctly. The same is true for other small groups led by Christians. Always teach and uphold God's truth.

As you are under Jesus Christ's authority as His servant-leader, you have the authority of "Content Guardian" to control the content of the discussion. You are serving the women in your group "in Jesus' name." That means you are acting under His commission and according to His character. Stay Christ-focused.

But remember to be humble and gracious in your leadership. Jesus is our best example. He demonstrated for us that you can maintain truth in a group setting while still being humble and gracious in the process. He will help you do that, too.

DIRECTING A CHRIST-FOCUSED DISCUSSION

A good discussion leader encourages all the women to contribute to the discussion and interact with one another while retaining control of the group and maintaining biblical integrity. That's a mouthful, isn't it?

Your group depends upon you to be the "thermostat." That means you set the tone for the group so that the group adjusts to that. This is better than being a "thermometer" who lets the group set the tone expecting you to adjust to the group. Be the thermostat.

If you are leading a Bible Study...

God wants you to follow His Son. But you won't follow someone you don't trust. You can't trust someone you don't know, and you cannot know Christ apart from His Word. (Rebecca Carrell, heartstrongfaith.com)

- **Learn from the study for yourself first.** Be a learner first before a discussion leader. Let Jesus teach you what He wants for you to know and do.

- **Plan ahead of time how you will lead the lesson.** One of your goals as the content guardian is to help others learn to feed themselves, too. Review your lesson and ask Jesus to help you make a plan. It's okay to make a plan. Just hand it to Him and give Him permission to change it. He will guide you through the Holy Spirit living inside you.

  As you open yourself to the Holy Spirit's leading, what you learn in your personal study time will be valuable to your group as you lead them through the discussion. Jesus will show you what the overall focus of your group discussion time should be, especially as you get to know the group members better.

  Remember, it's good to say, "Lord Jesus, I can't do this on my own. I will trust you to do this through me." Then, watch what He does!

- **Always read aloud the main Bible passage(s) that are the focus of the lesson.** If you just read the study questions and your answers, then your discussion is focused on human words rather than on God's revealed Word and your response to that. You can't assume that everyone has already read the Bible passages before coming to the group. It is better to skip questions and read the Bible passages than the other way around.

- **Encourage everyone to learn from the lesson on their own.** You want them to discover treasures from God's Word during the week, taking time to complete the lesson, and then to share with each other what they have learned.

  Sometimes I will read a question then say, *"What did you learn from this as you did your lesson?"* This reinforces that they would learn more from doing their lessons before coming to the group.

For all groups...

- **Ask if anyone feels comfortable reading aloud.** If So call on them to read the Bible verses and/or discussion questions. If you sense someone prefers not to be called on (or she has told you so), honor that request. Mark the application/share questions clearly. Read those yourself, especially if it asks a woman to reveal personal information.

- **Use any provided questions to get the discussion going.** Then, help direct it to encourage interaction among the group members. *"How would some of you answer this question?" "What do you all think about that?" "Does anyone else feel that same way?" "What might this look like in a person's life?"* Encourage the women to want to hear what the others have to say about the topic, not just what you say.

- **Limit your own talking** except to lead the discussion and to direct it or enhance it with something amazing that you learned from the Lord. We learn so much on our own as we prepare to lead a lesson. It's okay to show you are a learner, too. Mark those answers you specifically want to share. **Silence is okay!** Count to 10 or more before jumping in! Let the women have time to think. Ask the question again, perhaps rephrasing it.

- **Affirm those who share, especially if they are normally quiet.** Say, *"Thank you, _____, for sharing that."*

- **Clarify the truth gently if the comment needs further explanation.** This is especially needed if what was said is not in the Bible text or is contrary to what the Bible says is true. I try to always point them back to what the Scripture actually says. You want them to see what is there not what they want it to say. Ask the Lord to prompt you whether or not to speak about the comment or just to let it go.

- **Diffuse critical remarks** to ensure emotional comfort. Redirect. Use humor. Try not to embarrass the guilty party.

- **Avoid getting bogged down on any one issue.** This is where you pay attention to any notes you made about possible rabbit trails in the lesson. Be aware of them. Stay focused on what you decide is best for the group. Keep the discussion moving along.

- **Avoid the role of "answer woman."** Assume you will get asked questions for which you don't know the answers. That's a given!

And it's okay. You are not expected to have all the answers. No one does!

Dwell on what you CAN know that is truth. It's okay to focus on what you do know and what you want the group to be confident in knowing related to the lesson. Avoid speculation just to come up with an answer. Humbly accept what you can't know or don't understand. Graciously say, *"I don't know."* If it's important enough, try to find out the answer or challenge her to look up the answer. Remember, as Content Guardian, stay focused on the lesson. Your group will appreciate that.

What have you seen a leader do to guard the content of a discussion well?

What happens when a leader doesn't do that?

CHALLENGES TO CHRIST-FOCUSED DISCUSSION

Those who don't do their lessons ahead of time

If you are leading a group that is doing a Bible study and has homework, It is not unusual for someone to not get the lesson done for that week. You can't control this. Expect some to not have their lessons finished. Don't let it annoy you. Encourage all the group members to come to the study anyway and learn as you read the Bible passages and discuss them together. Perhaps that will generate a desire to carve out time to do the lesson at home.

Realize that some people are so busy with work, school, and family, that they have little time to do another thing for themselves. It could be just the season of life. They want to be part of your group. Keep encouraging them to feed themselves from God's Word, even if they only do the first page of the lesson. Do something. If this is the majority of your group, choose a shorter Bible study that can be done in one sitting. Make it easier for them to be successful.

However, some women routinely come to a study without doing the lesson yet freely participate in the discussion, giving their own opinions. As Content Guardian, you have the authority to keep referring back to the biblical text and look at what it says. Include her in the observation questions. Keep encouraging her to discover God's truth and point out the value of doing so. Ask the Lord to give her a desire to learn for herself. Ask Him for help in reaching her heart and her mind.

If you think she feels insecure about doing a Bible Study lesson, offer to get together and work through a study with her. Perhaps she's intimidated into thinking she can't do it on her own.

The temptation to "fix" each other's problems

When a woman in your group starts opening up about an issue she has and challenge she is facing, the other group members are often tempted to jump in and "fix it" for her. **Don't let this happen!** That is not good for community building.

It is not their job to give opinions or advice on how to fix each other. It's not your job to do that, either, or to be the "counsellor." That belongs to Jesus.

Tell them up front, *"We are not going to try to fix each other's issues. We will be good listeners and commit to pray for the Lord to work."*

You can also say, *"When you share your own lives and how Jesus has helped you, the others in your group will hear that. If they want to ask you questions about it, get together with them later."* This prevents group "counselling."

Also, keep the group from probing into personal and delicate family situations. You know how quickly that happens, even when someone mentions a prayer request. Don't let this happen, either.

As the leader, point everyone to depend on Jesus to show them a way out of any challenge. You will have to keep reminding them and yourself not to jump in and "fix it." **Stop and pray whenever the door is open for doing this.** Ask the Lord to take it upon Himself. Thank Him for doing that. Then, move along the lesson discussion.

STAY FOCUSED ON CHRIST

You are under Jesus Christ's authority as His servant-leader. You have the authority of "Content Guardian" to control the content of the discussion. You are serving the women in your group "in Jesus' name," acting under His commission and according to His character. Your group will be best served when you stay Christ-focused more than focused on you or each other. The strongest groups are those with community built around the truth of God and the love of Christ in their lives.

Remember that you don't know how long any woman will be in your group. People move all the time. By helping every woman to learn to rely on Christ more in their lives, you are helping them to stay strong regardless of what life changes may occur. Lead your lesson with that in mind, aiming for the heart and each one's relationship with Christ.

Prayer: Pray for yourself to stay Christ-focused and Christ-dependent as a leader. Ask Jesus to help you be humble and gracious in your leadership. Ask Him to help you maintain truth in a group setting while still being humble and gracious in the process. Ask Jesus to help you respond graciously to these challenges. Depend on Him to show you what to do. He is faithful!

Christ-Given Commission

Commissioned to Be Disciple-makers

Before returning to heaven after His resurrection, Jesus said to His followers:

> *All authority in heaven and on earth has been given to Me. Therefore go and MAKE DISCIPLES of all nations, baptizing them in the name of the Father and of the Son and of the Holy Spirit, and teaching them to obey everything I have commanded you. (Matthew 28:18-19)*

This is the commission to all believers. And our commission has a two-fold purpose.

First, you and I are to follow Him as His disciples. A disciple is an active follower or learner. To follow Jesus as His disciple means that you make the choice to learn from Jesus through what is taught in the Bible and apply those teachings to your life in obedience to Him. That's what you do to grow as a Christian. That's what you bring to your group.

Even more than that, you are commissioned to live for Him as a disciple-maker. That sounds scary, but it isn't. A disciple-maker simply reaches others for Christ, builds them up in the faith, and helps them reach their friends for Christ. That's what small group leaders do.

Thankfully, our Lord doesn't leave us on our own to do that disciple-making stuff in our lives. He gives His life to us in a powerful way through the Holy Spirit present in our lives. Our response is to live dependently on His power by faith.

As a small group leader, you have the opportunity to pursue disciple-making as you minister to the women of your small group, and you can encourage them to become disciple-makers as well.

FISHING POOLS FOR NEW DISCIPLES

Small groups are fishing pools for new disciples. They attract new Christians as well as those who have been believers for years but have never been discipled. As we mentioned earlier, non-Christians are attracted to small groups because they are seeking truth, understanding, or fellowship. A small group is a great opportunity to help someone grow in their relationship with Jesus and in His truth.

As you pay attention to your group members, you should recognize those who have yet to trust Christ. As you love them and listen to them, remember that their greatest need is a relationship with Jesus Christ.

You have two very powerful tools to introduce her to Jesus that cannot be stopped. You have (1) the gospel **facts** and (2) the story of your own **experience** validating the power of the gospel. People can reject the facts of the gospel and even its logic, but it is very hard to argue with someone about their experience of the gospel. Every Christ-focused small group leader should prepare to use those two powerful tools as needed in a group.

Sharing the gospel message

The gospel message is simple. God loves her and wants a relationship with her. But sin separates her from God and prevents that relationship. So God sent His Son to die for her sin. He offers complete forgiveness and salvation to her. All she must do is believe in Jesus Christ. Then, she begins a relationship with God as His adopted child. We covered this in Chapter One "Christ Is Our Focus."

If you need a tool to help you share the gospel message in your conversation with anyone, check out the ones we have provided in the RESOURCES section.

Practice the gospel message until you know it well. The idea is that when the opportunity comes up in conversation, you will be ready to share the gospel without stressing about remembering the "details."

If your group member trusts in Christ, introduce her to the group as their new sister in Christ. Lead a celebration of her new life.

Write out the simple gospel message below as you would share it with someone.

Sharing your faith story

Jesus Christ died for you…so He could give His life to you…so He could live His life through you. It's His story in your life. Only you know it. You can share it.

Think through what you might say if given 5 minutes in a conversation. As you review your lesson and make a plan for leading the discussion, consider where you could easily and quickly share part of your story.

What has Jesus done in your life? What is it like to have a relationship with God? Where have you learned to trust Him? How do you know He is real and what you have learned is true?

If you grew up in the church and stayed faithful to Jesus for the most part until now, you have the story every parent of young children wants to hear! What influenced you to stay faithful?

Remember what your life was like before you trusted in Christ. Or perhaps you trusted in Christ as a child, but later you made the choice to follow Him as His disciple.

Look in the RESOURCES section for tools that will help you share your faith story, especially "Create a 3-Word Story" and "Prepare Conversation Transitions." You will also find a worksheet to write a longer version of your faith story. Then, you can use the "Screen Your Language" ideas to check for "churchy" words. As hard as this seems, pare your story down to 5 minutes, or at least parts of it.

If you can give opportunity for your group members to share their 5-minute faith stories as a group activity, do so. Share the tools in the RESOURCES section with them ahead of time. Do the sharing during group time where it fits in with the lesson, or plan a group get together over dinner or dessert where there is plenty of time for each one to share her story.

If given the opportunity by the Holy Spirit to briefly share with an unbeliever about your relationship with Jesus, what would you say in less than 5 minutes? Consider two ways that knowing Jesus has made a difference in your life, given you hope, restored something lost, etc.

GROWING DISCIPLES

> *Meanwhile a Jew named Apollos, a native of Alexandria, came to Ephesus. He was a learned man, with a thorough knowledge of the Scriptures. He had been instructed in the way of the Lord, and he spoke with great fervor and taught about Jesus accurately, though he knew only the baptism of John. He began to speak boldly in the synagogue. When Priscilla and Aquila heard him, they invited him to their home and explained to him the way of God more adequately. (Acts 18:24-26)*

This is a great example of someone in leadership listening to what is being shared in a group setting, realizing that the person sharing is lacking some beneficial information, and personally discipling that person so he could influence others more effectively.

Since your group may contain mature Christians with tons of Bible knowledge alongside those who have limited Christian understanding, it is very important that you pay attention and come alongside them as needed. This is being a Christ-focused leader.

Pay attention.

You cannot assume that woman sitting next to you in your small group knows who she is in Christ. Listen to what she says. She may not even be a believer yet. She may be a new believer. She may be a long-time believer who has never been discipled and feels ignorant compared to others.

What if her answer reveals she doesn't know the truth? Maybe she is leaving blanks because she doesn't know how to do a study or can't figure out how to answer the question. Many Bible studies are written using one particular translation, so the question wording often reflects that. If she doesn't use the same translation, she may not know how to get the answer.

Come alongside her.

If you catch that she's new to Bible study, church, and/or doesn't know much, invite her somewhere to visit—maybe in your home or any place where you can be together and have enough quiet to discuss. Find out what her background is, what she already knows, and what she'd like to know. If she's interested in meeting with you one-on-one to get more established in her faith, agree on a first time to get together.

- **If she is just new to Bible study:** Offer to help her work through 1-2 Bible study lessons until she feels more comfortable with the process. Or, ask another group member to do this.

- **If she is a new Christian who doesn't know much yet:** Anyone who trusts in Christ needs to be discipled as a new believer. Be sure that you or someone you trust will meet with her to walk her through a new believer's guide such as *A Fresh Start* by Melanie Newton or other books designed for anyone new to the Bible. This will give her roots in the Christian faith.

- **If she has been a Christian for years but was never discipled:** Ask, "What do you already know? What do you want to know? What do you know about Christ? Do you know your identity in Christ? What do you know about living by the Spirit?" Many people in our churches don't know what that is.

  You can take her through *Graceful Living* by Melanie Newton. This will firmly establish her in her identity in Christ, Christ's finished work on the cross, what the resurrection means for her now, and how to live by the Spirit.

Encourage mature group members to do the same.

If you have several mature believers in the group and several new believers, encourage the mature Christians to pay attention and come alongside at least one younger believer in the group. Follow the same procedures as above. Encourage the women to be doing this outside the group as well with those in their sphere of influence who need to be more firmly established in their faith.

Why is it important to come alongside someone in your group who is struggling or lacking truth in her life rather than assuming she will "catch up" just by being in the group?

What did someone use to disciple you as a young believer?

PREPARE FUTURE LEADERS

Identify the woman in your group who demonstrates a greater level of spiritual interest and commitment to your group who might also be challenged to become a small group leader herself. You, in essence, help her develop as a leader who is capable of ministering to others.

Give her some responsibility within the group and lead her to rely on Christ to accomplish it. Challenge her to reach out to at least one other member of the group in the ways described above for disciple-making. Pray for her regularly. Enjoy your new relationship and leave the results up to the Holy Spirit! Then, watch what He does!

STAYING FOCUSED ON CHRIST

By faith, you can be a disciple-maker as Jesus commissioned you to be. You can do this in your personal life and small group ministry. Disciple-making is a lifestyle, not a program. It's investing your life in your two-fold purpose as a believer in Christ.

You can be a disciple-maker at any age or stage of life. Someone around you needs to know Jesus or needs to know Him better. And you can be confident that whatever Jesus calls you to do, He empowers you to do through His Spirit. Say "yes" and jump in with both feet!

As a Christ-focused small group leader, be onboard with your commission as a disciple-maker for Him!

Prayer: Submit yourself to the Lord to be a disciple-maker for Him. Ask Him to show you the women in your group whom He wants you to disciple in particular. Ask Him to lead the mature Christians in your group to join in discipling the younger Christians. Praise Him for the privilege of joining Him in His work.

Resources

Resources to help you lead

1. Group Meeting Location Details

2. DISC Dimensions of Behavior

3. Small Group Guidelines

4. Inductive Bible Study

5. Ways to Explain the Gospel

6. Create a 3-Word Faith Story

7. Prepare Conversation Transitions

8. "My Faith Story" Worksheet

9. Screen Your Language

GROUP MEETING LOCATION DETAILS

1. Know the physical address and phone contact of your group meeting location.

Address: _____

Phone contact: _____

2. Know where to find needed equipment: first aid kits, AED (defibrillator), and fire extinguishers.

First aid kit: _____

AED: _____

Fire extinguisher: _____

3. Know where to find medically trained personnel within your group or ministry, especially those trained in CPR.

Medically trained person nearby: _____

4. Know where to find safe areas from your meeting room in case of fire (generally outside the building) or a weather emergency (interior room away from windows).

Fire: _____

Severe weather: _____

5. Know what to tell parents about meeting their children during a fire or severe weather emergency.

Safe area to meet children: _____

DISC DIMENSIONS OF BEHAVIOR

As you read through the DISC information below, notice how the information can help you in your small group ministry to enhance communication and teamwork as well as resolve conflict with others.

D = Fast-Paced and Task-Oriented; Dominant, Direct and Active

The "D" behavior tendency describes those whose emphasis is shaping their environment by overcoming opposition to accomplish results.

- A "D" is comfortable at solving problems, making quick decisions, and accepting challenges.

- A "D" struggles with impatience, overlooking cautions, and being demanding of others.

- Motivate a "D" by emphasizing goals and results and soliciting their help to accomplish them. Let them have control of something. Get in their face and challenge them. "I bet you can't do…" often works.

- Resolve conflict with a "D" by being direct, ask what is necessary for a "win-win" solution while avoiding "who's right or wrong" debates.

I = Fast-Paced and People-Oriented; Influence, Interested and Lively

The "I" behavior tendency describes those whose emphasis is shaping their environment by influencing or persuading others.

- An "I" usually speaks with ease so is valuable as a lecturer, greeter, and making people feel very comfortable.

- An "I" struggles with sensitive feelings, being unorganized, and telling long stories.

- Motivate an "I" by appreciating their efforts in front of others, letting them have fun, and putting them in a position of influence over others.

- Resolve conflict with an "I" by assuring her of your love and relationship, dealing with the issues without personal criticism, and caring about her feelings.

S = Slow-Paced and People-Oriented; Steady & Cooperative

The "S" behavior tendency describes those whose emphasis is on cooperating with others to carry out the task.

- An "S" is a dependable team player, will do a job consistently week after week, and is a good listener.

- An "S" struggles with resisting change, soft-heartedness, and procrastination.

- Motivate an "S" by emphasizing the need of the group, minimizing conflict, and doing things together.

- Resolve Conflict with an "S" by emphasizing what is best for the group or team, being calm and friendly, and offering a comfortable solution.

C = Slow-Paced and Task-Oriented; Conscientious & Correct

The "C" behavior tendency describes those whose emphasis is on working conscientiously within existing circumstances to ensure quality and accuracy.

- A "C" is valuable at organizing information, problem solving, and maintaining accuracy.

- A "C" struggles with getting bogged down in detail, hesitancy to reveal true feelings, and taking a long time to make decisions.

- Motivate a "C" by emphasizing quality in a task, giving her time to do things right, and working closely with her so she knows her work will be approved.

- Resolve conflict with a "C" by stating the issue calmly and logically; ask what is necessary for a "win-win" solution, and giving her time to think about the situation. Be sure to schedule a follow-up discussion.

What did you learn that will help you relate to someone whose behavioral tendencies are different from yours?

SMALL GROUP GUIDELINES

Having guidelines for attendance and discussion helps to build community within your group. You can use the following guidelines to maintain a safe environment for your group members to learn together.

1. **Attend consistently** whether your lesson is done or not. You'll learn from the other women, and they want to get to know you.

2. **Set aside time** to work through the study questions. The goal of Bible study is to get to know Jesus. He will change your life.

3. **Share your insights** from your personal study time. As you spend time in the Bible, Jesus will teach you truth through his Spirit inside you.

4. **Respect each other's insights**. Listen thoughtfully. Encourage each other as you interact. Refrain from dominating the discussion if you tend to be talkative. ☺

5. **Celebrate our unity** in Christ. Avoid bringing up controversial subjects such as politics, divisive issues, and denominational differences.

6. **Maintain confidentiality.** Remember that anything shared during the group time is not to leave the **group** (unless permission is granted by the one sharing).

7. **Pray for one another** as sisters in Christ.

8. **Get to know the women** in your group. Please do not use your small group members for solicitation purposes for home businesses, though.

INDUCTIVE BIBLE STUDY

The inductive process is the best approach for doing Bible Study. The process consists of three actions: Observation, Interpretation, and Application. Ask the Holy Spirit to guide you through the process.

Start with the "ABCs"

Author—Who wrote the passage?

Background—When did the author live? In what culture?

Context—How does the passage fit in with what comes before and after it?

Observation: what's actually there

This step answers the question, **"What does the passage say?"** Read and reread the passage. Read it in another version of the Bible if available. Look for the facts: Who? What happened? What was taught? When? Where? How? Why? What is repeated? This is where you discover what the biblical text is saying.

Interpretation: the author's intended meaning

This step answers the question, **"What does it mean?"** What is the author's intended meaning in this passage? What is God trying to communicate through the writer? What did the people of that day understand? What do other scriptures say about the ideas in this passage? These "cross references" are usually found in the margins of Bibles or in footnotes.

Use Bible study aids to get a clearer meaning of the passage as needed: commentaries, Bible dictionaries, concordances, *Blue Letter Bible* or an online Bible study guide for the text, subject, or person you are studying. Use a dictionary to define words.

Application: making it personal

This step answers the question, **"How does this apply to me today?"** What is the Holy Spirit saying to us in this passage? What is one way I can apply the heart of this passage to my life? What will I do differently because of what I've learned?

WAYS TO EXPLAIN THE GOSPEL

The following scripts will help you learn how to share the gospel with someone whenever the opportunity arises. Ask: "Has anyone introduced you to Jesus so you could know Him? May I?"

Good News, Bad News (evantell.org)

1. The Bible contains both bad news and good news. The bad news is something about you and me, and the good news is something about God. Let's discuss the bad news first.

   Bad News #1—We are all sinners. Romans 3:23

   Bad News #2—The penalty for sin is death. Romans 6:23

2. Since there was no way you could come to God, the Bible says that God decided to come to you.

   Good News #1—Christ died for you. Romans 5:8

   Good News #2—You can be saved through faith in Christ. Ephesians 2:8-9

3. Is there anything keeping you from trusting Christ right now? Would you like to pray right now and tell God you are trusting His Son as your Savior?

Bridge to Life (Navigators)

Use paper and pen for drawing the parts of the gospel message.

1. The Bible teaches that God loves all humans and wants them to know him. John 10:10; Romans 5:1

2. But humans have sinned against God and are separated from God and his love. Draw a chasm. This separation leads only to death and judgment. Romans 3:23; Isaiah 59:2

3. But there is a solution. Draw a bridge. Jesus Christ died on the cross for our sins (the bridge between humanity and God). 1 Peter 3:18; 1 Timothy 2:5; Romans 5:8

4. Only those who personally receive Jesus Christ into their lives, trusting Him to forgive their sins, can cross this bridge. Everyone must decide individually whether to receive Christ. John 3:16; John 5:24

Four Spiritual Laws (Cru)

1. God loves you and offers a wonderful plan for your life. John 3:16; 10:10

2. Humans are sinful and separated from God. Thus, they cannot know and experience God's love and plan for their lives. Romans 3:23; Romans 6:23

3. Jesus Christ is God's only provision for humanity's sin. Through Jesus, you can know and experience God's love and plan for your life. Romans 5:8; John 14:6

4. We must individually receive Jesus Christ as Savior and Lord, and then we can know and experience God's love and plan for our lives. John 1:12; Ephesians 2:8-9

Using John 3:16

For God so loved the world that he gave his one and only Son, that whoever believes in him shall not perish but have eternal life.

1. **God loves:** *"For God loves you (name) so much..."* God is real. He loves you with an unconditional, never-ending love. He created you to have a relationship with Him. But we can't experience this loving personal relationship because of sin in our lives. Sin is disobeying God. It puts a barrier between us and a holy God. No matter how hard you try, you cannot be good enough on your own to overcome this sin barrier. The penalty for sin is death. God's love had a plan...

2. **God gave:** *"God gave His one and only Son"* Jesus to live as a human without sin and then to take the penalty for our sin on Himself when He died on the cross. He was buried as a dead man then raised from the dead to be alive again so our sins could be forgiven.

3. **We believe God's love:** *"Whoever believes in Him."* Faith is trust. God asks that we trust in His plan, admit our sin and desire for a relationship with Him. Accept what Jesus did on the cross for us out of love.

4. **We receive what God gave:** *"Shall not perish but have eternal life."* To perish means to die separated from God and His love for you. Eternal life means you can enjoy a forever-family relationship with God and promise of living securely with Him now and after your life on earth ends. When offered a gift you want, you take it and say thank you. It's forever yours. Is there anything keeping you from trusting in Jesus right now?

Here's a prayer anyone can pray to receive Christ:

Thank you, God, for loving me and for sending Your Son Jesus to die for my sins. I trust in Jesus Christ to be my personal Savior and turn my entire life over to You. Thank you for rescuing me and loving me as your child. Amen.

CREATE A 3-WORD FAITH STORY

1. Choose the first word to describe your life, feelings, situation, or thoughts **before trusting in Christ**. *Examples: angry, independent, manipulative, miserable, hopeless, empty, addicted, me-centered, restless, striving, confused, insecure, worried.*

   WORD #1 _____

2. Choose the second word to describe **how you came to trust in Christ**. *Examples: creation, studied, concert, grew, Bible, friend, trouble, observation, evangelist, spouse, loved, teacher, parent.*

   WORD #2 _____

3. Choose the third word to describe your life, feelings, situation, or thoughts **since trusting in Christ**. *Examples: peaceful, loving, trusting, freedom, servant, hopeful, compassionate, confident.*

   WORD #3 _____

Using your three words, create 1-2 sentences for each word—just a brief explanation how each word relates to your story. 3 words + 1 or 2 sentences per word = 3–6 sentences to tell your story. How simple is that! Here's an example:

> Before coming to faith in Jesus Christ, I was **ME-CENTERED** and thought I was in control of my life. If I wanted something to happen (specifically, get a boyfriend!), I had to make it happen! My sisters came to faith before I did, and through them I saw a lack in my own life. When I heard an **EVANGELIST** on TV present the gospel, I realized what the lack was. It was a Person, Jesus Christ, and I prayed and asked Him to forgive my sins. Now, I am most blessed in relinquishing control to Him, **TRUSTING** Him with all my heart, leaning not on my own understanding, acknowledging Him in all my ways and allowing Him to straighten my paths. ("Create Your Own 3-Word Testimony!" evantell.org)

Create your own 3-word faith story:

PREPARE CONVERSATION TRANSITIONS

Consider simple statements or questions you could include in conversation that could lead into your sharing your story. Then, be ready for openings in the conversation where you can share simple statements of what God has done in your life. Give her a peak into the life you have in Christ. Create curiosity for more.

Use these examples of common topics and finish out what you would say.

- Corruption, evil and sin – "Though I am not guilty of that particular sin, I am just as guilty of…

_____

- Community – "Part of why I am so passionate about authentic community is because we are created by God to live in real community, first of all with Him. And I've experienced this…

_____

- Family – "I am so glad God cares even more about my family than I do. What would I do without Him helping me to…

_____

- Something good happened – "God has been so kind to you in that. I see His kindness to me every day…

_____

- High expectations – "I am so glad God doesn't expect perfection from me. What a relief it was for me to know…

_____

- Other –

_____

Prayer: Ask Jesus to give you boldness and opportunity to use these soon.

"My Faith Story" Worksheet

Option 1: Specific turning point leading to salvation

Two options are given for writing your story. If you became a Christian as a teen or adult so that you remember what life was like before knowing Him, use Option 1. If you became a Christian as a child and stayed faithful to Him through the years, choosing to become His disciple as a teen or adult, use Option 2. If you trusted Christ as a child, then drifted far away only to come back later in life, use Option 1 focusing on what caused you to come back to Him and choose to be His disciple now.

Before you trusted in Christ

Although the tendency is to spend most of the time on your "before Christ" experience, only give enough information so the women know why you needed Christ in your life. Tell them what you needed so that some may identify with you.

Identify what your life was like. What were your attitudes, needs, and/or problems? From what did you get your security or happiness? How did those areas begin to disappoint you? To what source did you look for security, peace of mind, or happiness? In what ways were your activities unsatisfying?

Find 2-3 words to describe what only Christ could fill or do in your life (e.g. loneliness, feelings of insignificance, anger, rejection).

Briefly share a personal example that captures the needs and attitudes from this time of your life as identified above.

How you came to know Christ (point of salvation)

Share when and how you first heard the gospel and/or were exposed to Christianity. What brought you to the place of being willing to listen? Who influenced you? How and when did you decide to follow Jesus? Describe how you felt, what truths you heard, what you thought about them, how you felt after you made the decision. Give the gospel in this section. Use 1 or 2 relevant scripture verses.

Your life after knowing Jesus

What conditions in your life before Christ has now been satisfied by a relationship with Him? What does it look like in your life to have a relationship with Christ? How long did it take before you noticed changes? What are your blessings? Where do you struggle? How do you depend on Him through those struggles? What difference does having Him in your life make during those times? Emphasize what you have learned about God's grace to you.

Briefly share a personal illustration that shows the wonderful difference that Christ has made in your life.

Wrap up by inviting them to trust in Christ as you did!

Write your five-minute faith story.

As you tell your story, what is the one big idea you want everyone to walk away remembering? This is your **main idea**—kind of like a theme. Some examples are: "Jesus satisfied my loneliness" or "To live with purpose is knowing Christ in my life." Think about those comments a woman might make that gives you an opening to tell this part of your story.

Whether you like to be spontaneous or need everything written down, it helps to script what you will say. It forces you to think through what you will say to maintain your main idea. It helps you to manage your allowed time.

Write it as you would speak it—shorter sentences, peppy words that are clear and simple. Use every day terminology. For example, instead of saying "my testimony," say "the story of my life." See "Screen Your Language" on page 78 for other alternatives. Include specific illustrations that give them snapshots of your life, not only general descriptions of your life events. Practice telling your story several times. Make eye contact with the listener to draw her into your story.

Write out your five-minute faith story. Remember only spend 30% of the time on your "before," just enough to have them identify with your need at that time. Spend another 30% on the decision time, and spend the rest of the time on what knowing Christ has done for you. Always end by inviting them to join your adventure.

Option 2: Believer to Christ-follower (disciple)

Those who trusted Christ as children often feel they "have nothing to tell" because they don't have a dramatic story. Yet, your story is the one every parent wants for their children! In the case of childhood believers, there occurs a later, mature decision to follow Christ as His disciple where more obvious life changes occurred. If you are in this category, therefore, focus on that later turning point in telling your story.

Although the tendency is to spend most of the time on your "before" experience, only give enough information so the women know why you needed Christ in your life. You want them to be able to identify with you.

Before you became Jesus' disciple

Identify what your life was like as a young Christian or living as just a believer not a disciple. Share when and how you first heard the gospel and/or were exposed to Christianity. What were your attitudes, needs, and/or problems? From what did you get your security or happiness?

Briefly share a personal example that captures the needs and attitudes from this time of your life as identified above.

What led you to become Jesus' disciple?

Share what brought you to the place of being willing to listen or of wanting to be more than just a believer. Who influenced you? How and when did you decide to follow Jesus? Describe how you felt, what truths you heard, what you thought about them, how you felt after you made the decision. Give the gospel in this section. Use 1 or 2 relevant scripture verses. Emphasize what you have learned about God's grace to you.

Your life after becoming Jesus' disciple

What conditions before this time has now been satisfied by a deeper relationship with Him? How long did it take before you noticed changes? What does it look like in your life to have this closer relationship with Christ? What are your blessings? Where do you struggle? How do you depend on Him through those struggles? What difference does having Him in your life make during those times? What remarkable thing has Jesus done in your life (or in the last three years)?

Briefly share a personal illustration that shows the wonderful difference that following Christ has made in your life.

Wrap up by inviting them to trust in Christ as you did!

Write your five-minute faith story.

As you tell your story, what is the one big idea you want everyone to walk away remembering? This is your **main idea**—kind of like a theme. "Jesus satisfied my loneliness" or "To live is knowing Christ in my life."

Whether you like to be spontaneous or need everything written down, it helps to script what you will say. It forces you to think through what you will say to maintain your main idea. It helps you to manage your allowed time.

Write it as you would speak it—shorter sentences, peppy words that are clear and simple. Use every day terminology. For example, instead of saying "my testimony," say "the story of my life." See "Screen Your Language" on page 78 for other alternatives. Include specific illustrations that give them snapshots of your life, not only general descriptions of your life events. Practice telling your story several times. Make eye contact with the listener to draw her into your story.

Write out your five-minute faith story. Remember only spend 30% of the time on your "before," just enough to have them identify with your need at that time. Spend another 30% on the decision time, and spend the rest of the time on what knowing Christ has done for you. Always end by inviting them to join your adventure.

SCREEN YOUR LANGUAGE

Adapted from *Stonecroft Ministries Speaker Workshop*

Unlearning the lingo

Many of the words we use to share our faith may be meaningless, too churchy or clichéd to the people we're attempting to reach. If you were an unbeliever, which words in the following would you have difficulty understanding?

> I heard the plan of salvation and was told that I needed to be saved. So I went forward to be born again. The Lord spoke to me and then opened the door of my heart to show me God's plan for my life. I learned to stand on God's word and began to walk with the Lord. I turned away from worldly things, and it has been such a blessing.

Instead of using churchy clichés, here are some alternatives.

Cliché	Alternative
Scripture or Bible verse	A place in the Bible where it says…
Born again, converted	Changed, transformed (with explanation)
Christian	Follower of Christ
Confess	Admit, agree with God
Found the Lord, got saved	Accept Christ, make a decision to follow Christ
Grace	God's totally unearned forgiveness
Gospel	God loves us and sent His Son so that we can find forgiveness and new life through Him
Know	Believe, trust, be certain
The Lord	God, Creator, Jesus
The Holy Spirit	God's Spirit, the Spirit of God
Praise	Thanking God for His greatness
Pray	Talk with God, ask God
Repent	To be sorry about wrongs and to turn from them to do right
Salvation, saved	Forgiven of wrongs and given eternal life
Savior	Jesus, God's Son, who forgave my wrongs and gave me eternal life
Sin, sinner	Acting against God's will and offending God's character; the wrong things that we do
Testimony	Telling my story
Witness	Tell, show

What could you use instead of these?

- Into my heart: _____
- Lord of my life: _____
- The Lord told me/spoke to me/directed me: _____
  _____

In most cases, you may want to avoid using theological words such as *justification* or the *sovereignty of God* unless you explain them well.

If you are praying with nonbelievers present, even with believers, be careful how often you address God by name in prayer. Prayer is simply talking to God. In normal speech, you wouldn't continually repeat someone's name, but many Christians think it necessary to mention God's name after every few words or so. This is disconcerting to non-Christians. Write out your prayer if this is a temptation for you.

Above all, be real and be normal.

Avoid Inappropriate Information.

- Use discretion in naming religions, churches, denominations, or cults.
- Avoid controversial issues such as doctrinal, political and social issues.
- Avoid derogatory remarks relating to any person, place, group, or issue.
- Stay away from promoting any project, campaign, business, cause, or financial need.
- Consider whether referring to any person, especially family members, could cause embarrassment or conflict. Ask permission before doing so.

Sources

1. DISC Dimensions of Behavior

2. "Free individual survey," accessed at gifts.churchgrowth.org

3. Heather Zempel, *Community Is Messy*,

4. Kenneth Boa, "The Gifts of the Spirit," accessed at Bible.org

5. Major Ian Thomas, *The Saving Life of Christ*

6. Melanie Newton, *A Fresh Start*

7. Melanie Newton, *Graceful Living*

8. Rebecca Carrell, heartstrongfaith.com

9. *Stonecroft Speaker Workshop*, sponsored by Stonecroft Ministries.

www.ingramcontent.com/pod-product-compliance
Lightning Source LLC
Chambersburg PA
CBHW070806120626
46557CB00002B/725